THE

GLENS OF

ROSS-SHIRE

THE GLENS OF
ROSS-SHIRE

A personal survey of the Glens of Ross-shire
for mountainbikers and walkers

by

Peter D. Koch - Osborne

CICERONE PRESS

MILNTHORPE, CUMBRIA, ENGLAND

©P.D. Koch-Osborne 2000
ISBN 1 85284 296 2

British Library Cataloguing-in-Publication Data.
A catalogue record for this book is
available from the British Library.

Through a clearing came the blaze of sun-
struck hills reflected in utterly calm water.
Its richness of varied colour gave it the likeness
of an ancient stained-glass window, but no
window ever glowed like that loch.
I had no more doubts about Glen Affric.
Its attributes were made manifest.
                                    W. H. Murray
                                    Undiscovered Scotland
                                    Diadem Books

Cover Pictures:- Loch Fannich
                      Loch Damh

Introduction

Access to the tracks on the following pages can rarely be regarded as an absolute right by the cyclist or walker. Almost all land is private and it is often only the good nature of the owners that allows us to travel unhindered over his land. In Scottish law the term trespass implies nuisance or damage. In practice sensible conduct removes any possibility of nuisance. Respect the grouse season (12 Aug to 10 Dec) and deer stalking (1 Jul to 20 Oct - stags and 21 Oct to 15 Feb - hinds). Your author has not once met with animosity in meeting 'keepers. Your good conduct will ensure continued access. Cyclists - stay on the trail and slow down!!

Conservation of the wild areas of Scotland is of paramount importance. Much has been written elsewhere but users of this guide must appreciate that the very ground over which you walk or cycle will be damaged if care is not taken. Please don't use a bike on soft peat paths and tread carefully on other than a stony track. Many of the tracks are in themselves an eyesore and any "development" can cause irreparable damage. Make sure, as walkers and cyclists, we encourage the conservation of our wilderness areas without the pressure of our activities causing further damage. In publishing this book a great deal of trust is placed upon you, the reader, to respect the needs of the region. If all you need is exercise - go to a sports centre! but if you appreciate the unique qualities of the wild places they are yours to enjoy..... carefully! Careless conduct not only damages what we seek to enjoy but, equally seriously, gives landowners good reason to restrict access.

<u>The Maps</u> on the following pages give sufficient detail for exploration of the glens but the Ordnance Survey Landranger maps of the region should also be used if the full geographical context of the area is to be fully appreciated. These maps and the knowledge of their proper use are essential if a long tour or cross country route is to be undertaken.

<u>The mountain bike</u>, or ATB - all terrain bike, has in the author's opinion been badly named. It does not belong on the high tops but is ideal in the glens covering at least twice the distance of the average walker, quietly, whilst still allowing a full appreciation of the surroundings and providing further exploration into the wilderness especially on short winter days. The bike must be a well maintained machine complete with a few essential spares as a broken bike miles from anywhere can be serious. Spare gear is best carried in strong panniers on good carriers. Poor quality bikes and accessories simply will not last. Front panniers help distribute weight and prevent "wheelies". Mud-guards are essential. Heavy rucksacks are tiring and put more weight onto one's already battered posterior! The brightly coloured "high profile" image of mountainbiking is unsuited to the remote glens. These wild areas are sacred and need treating as such.

<u>Clothing</u> for the mountainbiker is an important consideration, traditional road cycling gear is un-suitable. High ankle trainers are best for summer, and light weight walking boots for winter cycling. A zipped fleece jacket with waterproof top and overtrousers with spare thin sweatshirts etc

should be included for easily adjusting temperature. The wearing of a helmet is a personal choice, it depends how you ride, where you ride and the value you place on your head! In any event a thin balaclava will be required under a helmet in winter or a thick one in place of a helmet. Good waterproof gloves are essential. Fingers and ears get painfully cold on a long descent at −5°C. Protection against exposure should be as for mountain walking. Many of the glens are as high as English hilltops. The road cyclists shorts or longs will keep legs warm in summer only. In winter walker's breeches and overtrousers are more suitable.

<u>Clothing</u> for the walker has had much written about it elsewhere. Obviously full waterproofs, spare warm clothing, spare food etc. should be included. In winter conditions the longer through routes should never be attempted alone or by the inexperienced.

<u>Mountainbikers and walkers</u> alike should never be without a good map, this book (!), a whistle (and knowledge of its proper use), compass, emergency rations, and in winter a sleeping bag and cooker may be included even if an overnight stop is not planned. Word of your planned route should be left together with your estimated time of arrival. The bothies must be left tidy with firewood for the next visitor. Don't be too proud to remove someone else's litter. Join the Mountain Bothies Association to help support the maintenance of these simple shelters. It should not be necessary to repeat the Country Code and the Mountain Bike Code, the true lover of the wild places needs peace and space - not rules and regulations.

River crossings are a major consideration when planning long or "through" routes virtually anywhere in Scotland. It must be remembered that snowmelt from the high mountains can turn what is a fordable stream in early morning into a raging torrent by mid afternoon. Walkers should hold on to each other, in three's, forming a triangle if possible. Rivers can be easier to cross with a bike, as the bike can be moved, brakes applied, leant on, then the feet can be re-positioned and so on. The procedure is to remove boots and socks, replace boots, make sure you can't drop anything and cross - ouch! Drain boots well, dry your feet and hopefully your still dry socks will help to warm your feet up. Snowmelt is so cold it hurts. Choose a wide shallow point to cross and above all don't take risks.

Ascents on a bike should be tackled steadily in a very low gear and sitting down wherever possible. While front panniers prevent "wheelies" sitting down helps the rear wheel grip. Standing on the pedals causes wheel slip, erosion, and is tiring. Pushing a laden mountainbike is no fun and usually the result of tackling the lower half of a climb standing up, in the wrong gear or too fast.

Descents on a bike can be exhilarating but a fast descent is hard on the bike, the rider, and erodes the track if wheels are locked. It is also ill-mannered towards others who may be just around the next bend.

Last but not least other users of the tracks need treating with respect - it may be the owner! Bad conduct can only lead to restricted access, spoiling it for us all.

The Maps 1

The maps are drawn to depict the most important features to the explorer of the glens. North is always at the top of each map and all maps, apart from the detail sketches, are to the same scale :- 1km or 0.6 miles being shown on each map. An attempt has been made to present the maps in a pictorially interesting way. A brief explanation of the various features is set out below :-

<u>Tracks</u>:- One of the prime objects of this book is to grade the tracks according to "roughness". This information is essential to the mountainbiker and useful to the walker. With due respect to the Ordnance Survey one "other road, drive or track" can take twice as long to cycle along as another yet both may be depicted in the same way. The author's attempt at grading is set out below:-

metalled road, not too many fortunately, public roads are generally included only to locate the start of a route.

good track, hardly rutted, nearly as fast as a road to cycle on but can be boring to walk far on. Most are forest tracks.

the usual rutted "Landrover" track, rough but all easily rideable on a mountainbike, not too tedious to walk on.

rough, very rutted track nearly all rideable, can be very rough even for walking. Either very stony or overgrown or boggy.

walker's path, usually over 50% is rideable and included especially as a part of a through route. Details given on each map.

<u>Relief</u> is depicted in two ways. The heavy black lines are now a commonly used method of depicting main mountain summits, ridges and spurs thus:-

Contour lines are also used, at 50m intervals up to about 600m. This adds "shape" to the glens as mapped and gives the reader an idea of how much climbing is involved. Reference to the gradient profiles at the start of each section compares the various routes:-

500m   550m   600m

<u>Crags</u> in the high mountains are shown thus:-   ....with major areas of scree shown dotted

<u>Rivers</u> generally "uncrossable" are shown as two lines whilst streams, generally "crossable" are shown using a single line. Note:- great care is needed crossing even the larger streams. Falling in can cause embarrassment at best, exposure or drowning at worst. Please don't take risks - besides you'd get this book wet !!

loch or lochan

<u>Buildings</u> and significant ruins are shown as a:- ■

<u>Bridges</u> are rather obviously shown thus:-
There are so many trees I wish there were an easier way of drawing them - but there isn't ! I'm fed up with drawing trees !!

etc etc.....

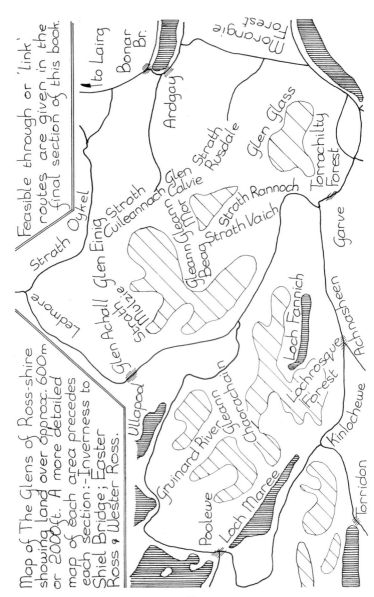

Map of The Glens of Ross-shire showing land over approx. 600m or 2000ft. A more detailed map of each area precedes each section:- Inverness to Shiel Bridge; Easter Ross & Wester Ross.

Feasible through or 'Link' routes are given in the final section of this book.

to Lairg

Bonar Br.

Morangie Forest

Ardgay

Glen Glass

Torrachilty Forest

Strath Oykel

Strath Cuileannach Glen Calvie

Glen Strath Rusdale

Strath Einig

Strath Rannoch

Gleann Mor

Gleann Beag Strath Vaich

Glen Achall

Ledmore

Strath Mulzie

Garve

Loch Fannich

Lochrosque Forest

Achnasheen

Ullapool

Gruinard River

Gleann Chaorachain

Loch Maree

Kinlochewe

Poolewe

Torridon

12

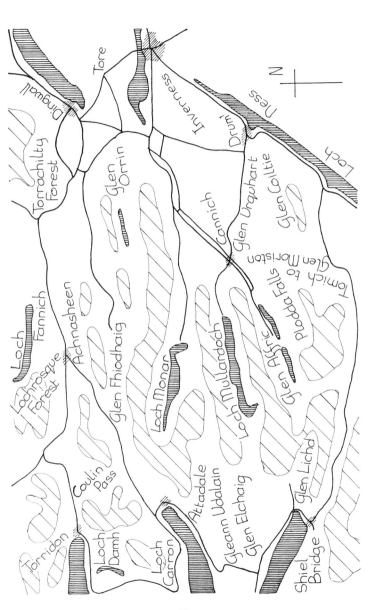

Inverness to Shiel Bridge

Inverness to Shiel Bridge

Access:- This region encompasses the southern extremities of this guide from west to east, bordered by the A87 Glen Shiel, A887 Glen Moriston and A82 Great Glen roads. Access is therefore easy from either the west (via Fort William and Loch Lochy) or from Inverness and the A9.

Accommodation:- Inverness has everything as has Drumnadrochit though in lesser quantity. Both the above do get very busy. West of these centres the two SYHA hostels at Loch Ness and especially Ratagan both provide a good base. Cannich hostel is very well placed for Affric and Plodda. Cluanie Inn is an hotel; b&b's thin out (indeed so does any habitation!) as one heads west, until Shiel Bridge is reached.

Geographical Features:- Almost the entire area is wild. Forest and moorland to the east, further west the glens narrow between shapely peaks. Glen Shiel is squeezed in between the Five Sisters Ridge and the South Kintail Ridge providing a dramatic approach to Shiel Bridge from the east. It is worth noting just how far west the east/west watersheds are.

Mountains:- The Five Sisters of Kintail, best viewed from near Ratagan Youth Hostel, are deservedly well known, with the South Kintail Ridge a close second place. A cluster of 3000 footers lies north and east of the Five Sisters and many of the tracks described can be used (by bike) to assist access to these fine hills. Further east the tops are rounded moors but exceptionally wild despite only just beating the 2000ft contour.

Rivers:- Most of the region drains to the east and these rivers suffer the usual Scottish characteristic of changing their name as they progress. The River Affric drains the north of the region, becoming the River Glass before changing its identity once again to the River Beauly on the final 'leg' to the Beauly Firth. The River Moriston flows out of Cluanie dam, having set out as the River Cluanie, on its way to Loch Ness. The River Coiltie also flows to Loch Ness down a glen of the same name, whilst the River Enrick drains Glen Urquhart. In the west the River Shiel makes its short dash for the sea and the even shorter River Croe drains Glen Lichd. There are no difficult river crossings unless spate conditions prevail.

Forests:- The main areas are Glen Affric, Plodda Falls and Glen Urquhart. Glen Affric is the best as it includes Scots Pine (your author's favourite tree), and thanks to planting these forests spill over to Plodda Falls and their combined access roads provide much good cycling. Glen Urquhart's forests are not as interesting but a good network of tracks lies alongside this peaceful glen, again giving good biking.

Lochs:- Loch Ness, complete with alleged monster, borders the region as does the dammed Loch Cluanie. Loch Beinn a Mheadhoin and Loch Affric are the most picturesque. A scattering of remote fishing lochans occupy the remote eastern moors. Loch Duich and the Beauly Firth flank the region, both linked by narrows to the open sea.

Emergency:- All routes start from populated areas but soon run out into wild country. Affric hostel is only open in summer but provides a haven. Always remember to let someone know where you are going – and report back.

Inverness to Shiel Bridge Routes 1

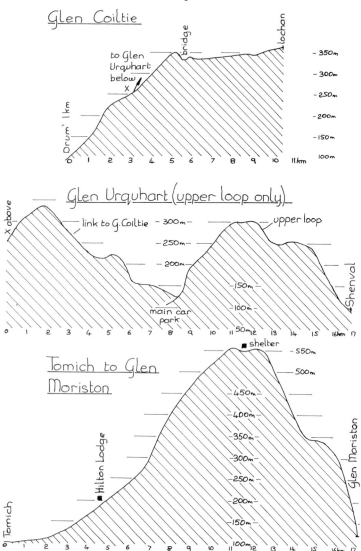

Glen Coiltie

- 350m
- 300m
- 250m
- 200m
- 150m
- 100m

bridge
lochan
to Glen Urquhart below X
Drum' 1km

0 1 2 3 4 5 6 7 8 9 10 11km

Glen Urquhart (upper loop only)

X above
link to G. Coiltie — 300m —
— 250m —
— 200m —
upper loop
— 150m —
— 100m —
main car park
— 50m —
Shenval

0 1 2 3 4 5 6 7 8 9 10 11 12 13 14 15 16km 17

Tomich to Glen Moriston

shelter
— 550m
— 500m
— 450m
— 400m
— 350m
— 300m
— 250m
— 200m
— 150m
— 100m

Hilton Lodge
Tomich
Glen Moriston

0 1 2 3 4 5 6 7 8 9 10 11 12 13 14 15 16km 17

18

Inverness to Shiel Bridge Routes 2

Plodda Falls

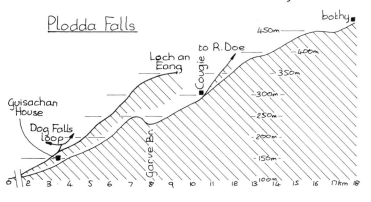

Glen Affric

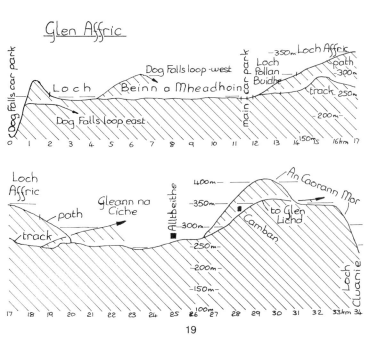

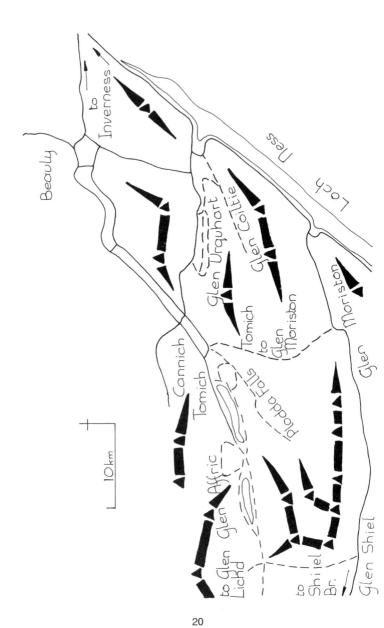

Once out of the woods the Glen Coiltie track becomes rough and progress on a bike is slow to the strange house-on-the-island at Loch Aslaich. The first couple of miles of track provide a connection between Drumnadrochit and the many tracks contouring above Glen Urquhart – see the next route. The distance to Loch Aslaich from the start of the track is 11 km or 7 miles (add 2 km or 1·5 miles from down-town Drum'.) There is no shelter in Glen Coiltie.

track joins Glen Coiltie to Glen Urquhart,

Contd Glen Urquhart 3

to Cannich & Beauly
to Inverness

Drumnadrochit

park

Contd Glen Coiltie 3

R. Coiltie

Lewiston

A82

to Fort Bill

track starts here

Divach

park for Divach falls

N

1 km

This hill leads to the Great Glen Cycle Route – an off-road mountainbike ride all the way to Fort William. See Book 6 "Invermoriston to Drumnadrochit 4", p 43.

21

Glen Coiltie 2

Only a few short miles from Drum', the Glen Coiltie track feels as remote as any – it touches on an almost completely unfrequented area of small fishing lochs.
A rough landscape of hill, rock outcrop and heather moor; and best of all, almost total solitude.

481m

Carn an t-Sluic Dhuibh 567m

1km

N

450

400

350

ford

River Coiltie

400

Strathan
Allt na Fiacail

450

Loch Aslaich

Continued opposite

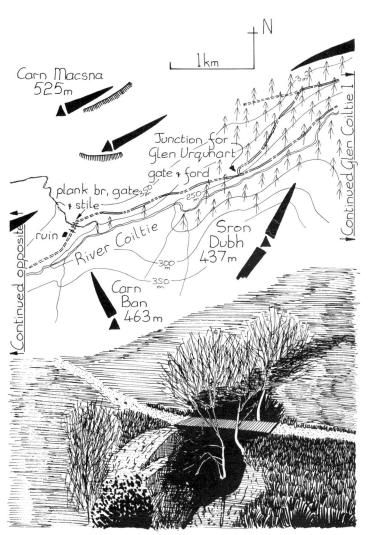

N

1km

Carn Macsna
525m

Junction for
Glen Urquhart

gate & ford

plank br, gate
& stile

ruin

River Coiltie

Sron
Dubh
437m

Carn
Ban
463m

250
m

300

350
m

Continued opposite

Continued Glen Coiltie 1

Glen Urquhart 1

The forest tracks above Glen Urquhart provide an endless, but not uninteresting, variety of routes for mountainbiking; contouring at various levels above the glen. Access is from the main car park with road connections at 'X'-the start of the Corrimony road; 'Y' Shenval; and 'Z' Shewglie. A further link connects Glen Urquhart with Glen Coiltie, the lower section of the latter track being good in contrast with its rough upper reaches. Distance is to choice, either a half day or a full day may be spent exploring these tracks. However a full day is required if the head of Glen Coiltie is to be included. There is no shelter other than the bus shelter at Shenval. Note the picnic table (below) at the western end of the forest.

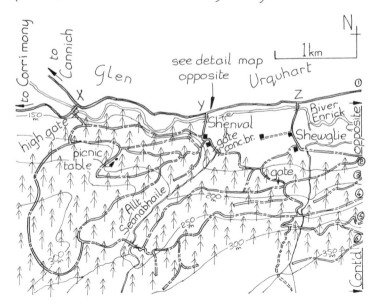

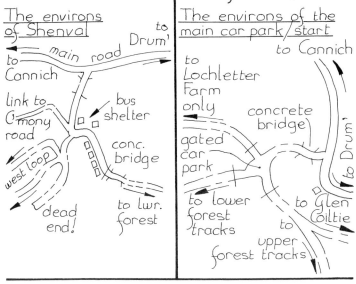

The environs of Shenval

to Drum'

main road

to Cannich

link to 'mony road

bus shelter

west loop

conc. bridge

dead end!

to lwr. forest

The environs of the main car park/start

to Cannich

to Lochletter Farm only

concrete bridge

gated car park

to lower forest tracks

to Glen Coiltie

to upper forest tracks

to Drum'

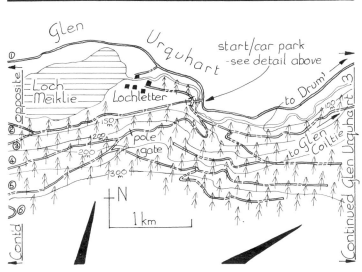

Glen Urquhart

start/car park - see detail above

to Drum'

Loch Meiklie

Lochletter

150 m

200 m

300 m

pole

gate

to Glen Coiltie

100 m

opposite

Contd

Continued Glen Urquhart 3

N

1 km

Glen Urquhart 3

Forestry - above
Loch Ness

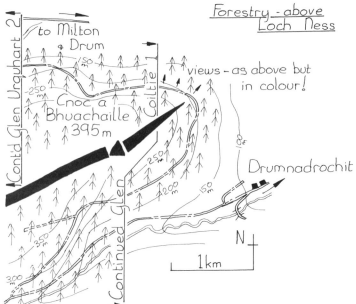

to Milton & Drum

Contd Glen Urquhart 2

Coiltie 1

Cnoc a Bhuachaille 395 m

150 m

250 m

views - as above but in colour!

100 m

Drumnadrochit

250 m

200 m

150 m

Continued Glen

350 m

300 m

N

1 km

The track from Tomich to Glen Moriston has many
similarities with the Corrieyairack Pass (Book 6).
It is part of the same military road; it crosses
a high pass; and unfortunately it is marred by
the same line of pylons as its better known twin.
The one-way distance is some 17km or 11miles,
and transport is needed at both ends of the
route for a complete traverse. There is
shelter near the summit of the pass in a
miserable concrete hut. The summit
lies at 560m so don't
underestimate the
amount of
climbing
required!

to Cannich

Knockfin Br.

Tomich

Guisachan

Loch na
Beinne Moire

Dog Falls
Loop

Continued Glen Affric 8

gate

gates

gates

monument

path
to Corrimony

403m monument

Guisachan Ho.

Guisachan
(ruin)

conc. br.

Loch a
Ghreidlein

gate

rough/overgrown

N

gate

1km

ends
in 500mts.

Hilton
Lodge

409m

X

gate

Y

Continued Plodda Falls 4

27

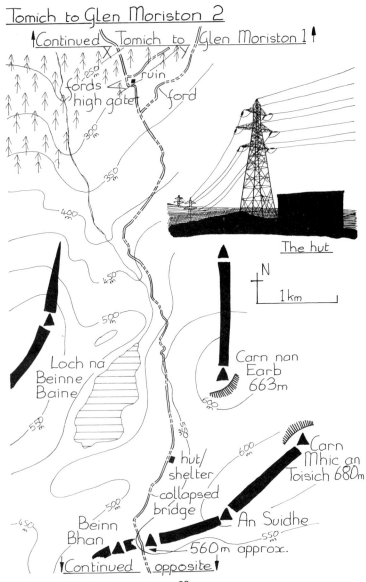

↑ Continued ↑ Tomich to Glen Moriston 1 ↑

fords
high gate
ruin
ford

250 m
300 m
350 m
400 m
450 m
500 m

The hut

N
1 km

Carn nan
Earb
663m

Loch na
Beinne
Baine

550 m

600 m
350 m

hut/
shelter

collapsed
bridge

600 m

Carn
Mhic an
Toisich 680m

An Suidhe

Beinn
Bhan

550 m

560m approx.

-450 m

500 m

↓ Continued ↓ opposite ↓

Tomich to Glen Moriston 3

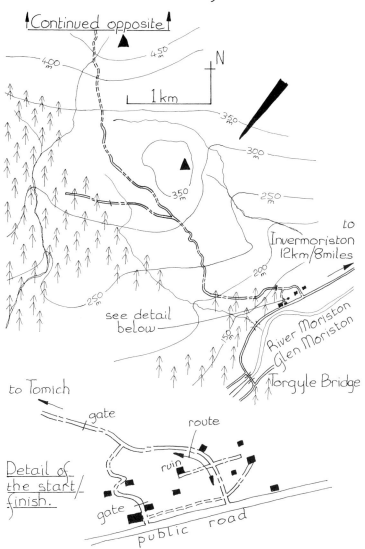

Continued opposite

450 m

400 m

N

1 km

350 m

300 m

350 m

250 m

to Invermoriston
12km/8miles

200 m

350 m

250 m

see detail below

150 m

River Moriston
Glen Moriston

Torgyle Bridge

to Tomich

gate

route

ruin

Detail of the start/finish.

gate

public road

Plodda Falls 1

The paths and tracks around Plodda Falls provide a superb area for walker and mountainbiker alike. Cyclists may prefer to start from Tomich or even Cannich, whilst walkers are better placed starting from the Plodda Falls car park, some 5km or 3 miles beyond Tomich.(Cyclists must watch for cars on this section). The tracks may be pursued to the old bothy, below, or via the hill path above Cougie to Glen Doe. Connections to Glen Affric are: a) via either 'leg' of the Dog Falls loop, or b) via the very rough path (no bikes!) opposite - note this involves crossing the Allt Garbh - not advisable if in spate. The less adventurous can enjoy just pottering around the Falls and the tracks around Tomich - with its further connection to Glen Moriston, see previous section. Approximate distances are given opposite. There is shelter in the boathouse at Loch nan Gillean.

Note!
No cycling on the paths in the immediate vicinity of Plodda Falls please!!

400 m
opposite

Continued

bothy

Loch an Squid

550 m
500 m

450 m

550 m

N

1 km

873 m

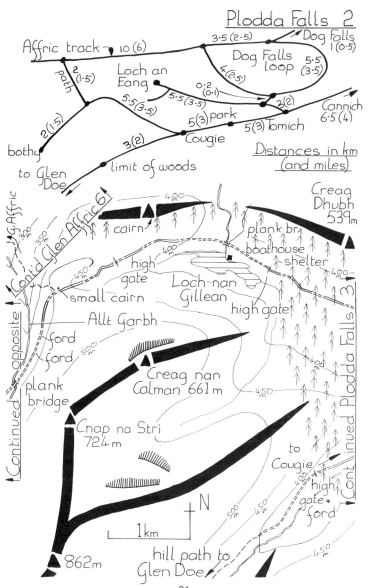

Plodda Falls 2

Affric track → 10 (6)

3.5 (2.5)

Dog Falls 1 (0.5)

Dog Falls Loop 5.5 (3.5)

path 2 (1.5)

Loch an Eang

4 (2.5)

0.2 (0.1)

5.5 (3.5)

5.5 (3.5)

2 (2)

Cannich 6.5 (4)

2 (1.5)

5 (3) park

5 (3) Tomich

bothy

3 (2)

Cougie

Distances in km (and miles)

to Glen Doe

limit of woods

G. Affric

Cont'd Glen Affric 6

300

350

400 m

cairn

Creag Dhubh 539 m

Continued opposite

350

450 m

high gate

400 m

plank br.

boathouse

shelter

400—

small cairn

Loch nan Gillean

high gate

Allt Garbh

ford

ford

500 m

400 m

plank bridge

Creag nan Calman 661 m

450

to Cougie

Cnap na Stri 724 m

400 m

Continued Plodda Falls 3

N

1 km

450 m

500 m

450 m

high gate

ford

862 m

hill path to Glen Doe

450 m

Plodda Falls 3

The track to Loch an Eang is worth pursuing for the viewpoint. The track ends at a high gate at which point take the boggy 'path' north west for 50 metres or so.

This point is only a few hundred metres from the Affric tracks. The path north from Loch an Eang, shown on the O.S. map, is non-existent or overgrown.

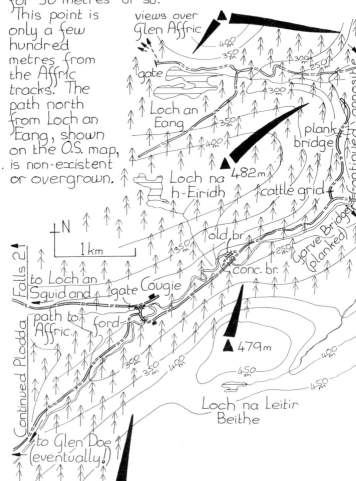

views over Glen Affric

400m
350m
300m
250m

gate

300m

Loch an Eang

350m

482m

Loch na h-Eiridh

plank bridge

cattle grid

Continued opposite

N

1 km

old br.

350m

250m

Garve Bridge (planked)

conc. br.

Falls 2

to Loch an Squid and

gate Cougie

path to Affric.

ford

300m
350m
400m

479m

450m

Loch na Leitir Beithe

400m

450m

Continued Plodda

to Glen Doe (eventually!)

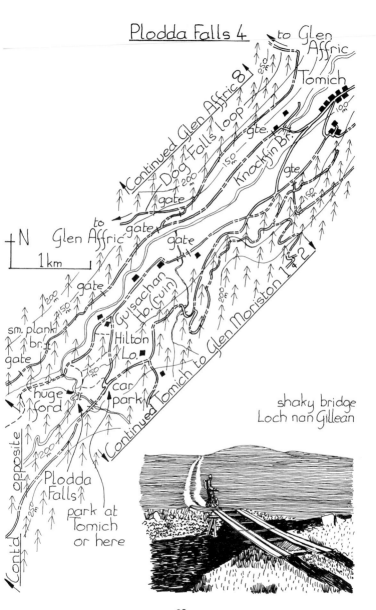

to Glen Affric

Tomich

Continued Glen Affric 8

Dog Falls loop

Knockfin Br.

250m

200m

150m

gte.

gte.

gte.

N
1 km

to Glen Affric

gate

gate

gate

gate

gate

Gulsachan Ho. (ruin)

Hilton Lo.

200m
150m

200m
150m

Continued Tomich to Glen Moriston 1 & 2

sm. plank br.

gate

huge ford

car park

250m
200m

Contd opposite

Plodda Falls

park at Tomich or here

shaky bridge
Loch nan Gillean

Glen Affric 1

Glen Affric is the best! The scenery is stunning, the mountainbiking is of the highest order, and the walking suits all standards from pottering-around-the-forest to mountaineering for several successive days - and all based on one glen! Lochs, rivers, waterfalls, and natural pine and birchwoods complete a perfect scene. The glen is popular, and therefore populated, on sunny summer weekends; a forest of signposts entices the non-adventurous away from the car. However, this somewhat spoon-fed scenery is soon left behind in the wilds of the upper glen which boast a youth hostel and a bothy. Connections exist to the west coast via Glen Lichd and to Glen Shiel and Glen Moriston via An Caorann Mor to Cluanie Inn (touching on some exciting routes detailed in Book 8). Lower down the glen is the easy Dog Falls

loop, with its connections to the tracks around Tomich and Plodda Falls; a ride around Loch Beinn a Mheadhoin; and a walker's Loop into Gleann nam Fiadh. Shelter is as shown on the page maps, and distances in km (and miles) shown on the page layout set out above.

Dog Falls car park

Dog Falls

L. Beinn a Mheadhoin

Loch Affric

L. Lichd

to G. Lichd

bothy

G. Shiel C.Inn

G. Moriston

to Plodda Falls

car park

YH

D.F. Loop

8   3.5 (2.5)   1 (0.5)
5.5 (3.5)
4 (2.5)

9 (6)   9 (6)

1.5 (1)

7 (4.5)   7.5 (4.5)   7

5 (3.5)   8.5 (5.5)   6

4   5

3

2

2.5 (1.5)   1 (0.5)

9 (5.5)

34

This map is not Glen Affric at all, but its connection to Glen Shiel and Glen Moriston via the Cluanie Inn.

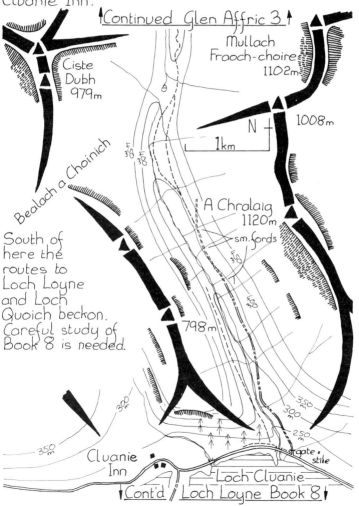

↑Continued Glen Affric 3↑

Mullach Fraoch-choire 1102m

Ciste Dubh 979m

1008m

N

1km

Bealach a Choinich

A Chralaig 1120m

sm. fords

South of here the routes to Loch Loyne and Loch Quoich beckon. Careful study of Book 8 is needed.

798m

Cluanie Inn

gate
stile

Loch Cluanie

↓Cont'd // Loch Loyne Book 8↓

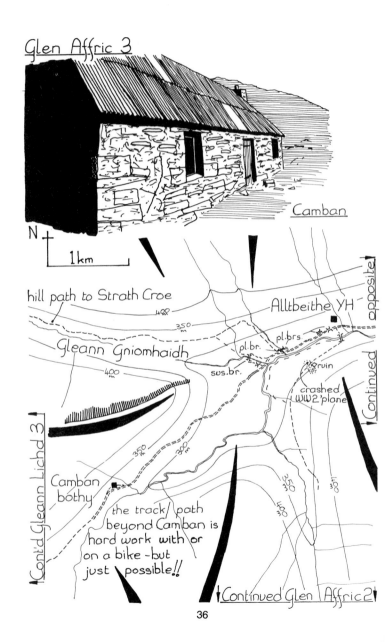

Camban

N
1km

hill path to Strath Croe

Alltbeithe YH

Gleann Gniomhaidh

pl.brs
pl.br.
sus.br.

ruin

crashed WW2 'plane

Continued opposite

Contd Gleann Lichd 3

Camban bothy

the track/ path beyond Camban is hard work with or on a bike -but just possible!!

Continued Glen Affric 2

36

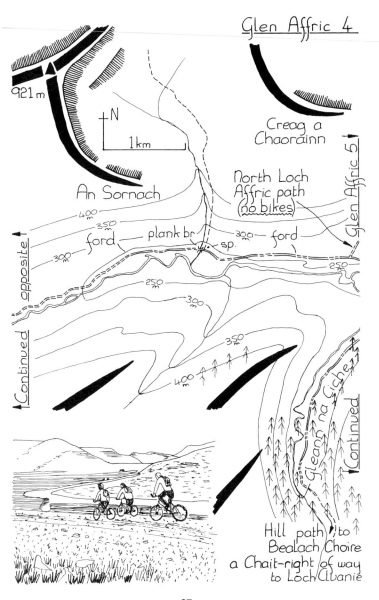

921 m

Creag a Chaorainn

An Sornach

North Loch Affric path (no bikes)

400 m
350 m
300 m
250 m

ford — plank br — sp. — ford

250 m

300 m

350 m

400 m

↑Continued opposite↑

Gleann na Ciche

Continued→

Hill path to Bealach Choire a Chait-right of way to Loch Cluanie

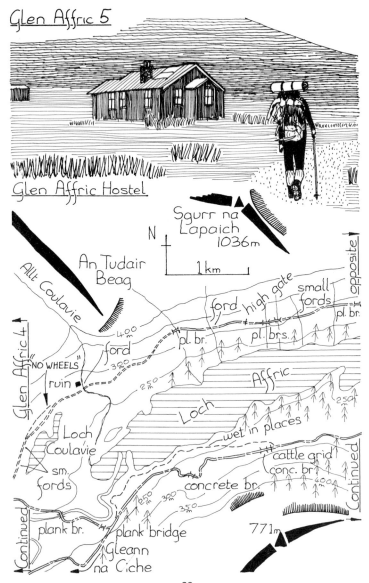

Glen Affric Hostel

Sgurr na Lapaich
1036m

N

1 km

An Tudair Beag

Allt Coulavie

Glen Affric 4

Affric

"NO WHEELS"

ford

ruin

ford

high gate

small fords

pl. br.

pl. brs.

pl. br.

400m

300m

250m

Loch

250m

opposite

Loch Coulavie

sm. fords

wet in places

cattle grid

conc. br.

concrete br.

400m

Continued

Continued

plank br.

plank bridge

150m

300m

350m

Gleann na Ciche

771m

Continued

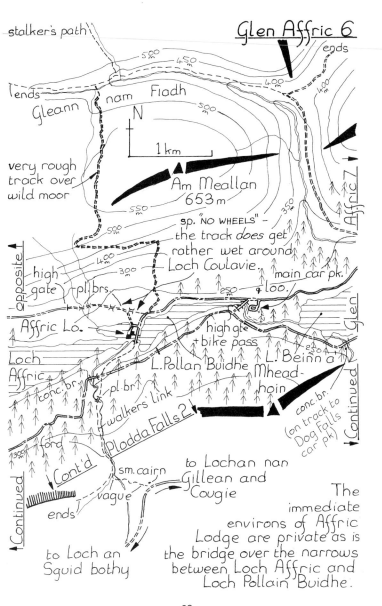

stalker's path

ends

500 m
450 m
400 m

ends

Gleann nam Fiadh

N

1 km

400 m

very rough
track over
wild moor

500 m

Am Meallan
653 m

550 m

350 m

Affric Z

sp. "NO WHEELS" –
the track *does* get
rather wet around
Loch Coulavie.

500 m

400 m

300 m

main car pk.

opposite

high
gate

pl. brs.

250 m

q loo.

Glen

Affric Lo.

high gte
+ bike pass

250 m

Loch

Affric

conc. br.

L. Pollan Buidhe

L. Beinn a
Mheadhoin

conc. br.
(on track to
Dog Falls
car pk)

Continued

Continued

pl. br.

walkers' link

1300 m

ford

Plodda Falls 2

Cont'd

sm. cairn

vague

to Lochan nan
Gillean and
Cougie

ends

Continued

to Loch an
Sguid bothy

The
immediate
environs of Affric
Lodge are private as is
the bridge over the narrows
between Loch Affric and
Loch Pollain Buidhe.

Glen Affric 7

This map depicts the link track between the Dog Falls loop and the upper Glen Affric tracks. Cyclists may of course use the quiet(ish) road from the head of the glen as a quicker return to Dog Falls car park – but who is in a hurry to leave Affric? The Dog Falls loop, opposite, provides a link to the extensive tracks around Plodda Falls, which in turn has off-road links much further afield. The area maps on Plodda Falls 2, page 31, and Glen Affric 1, page 34, give an insight into the many possibilities. Several days are needed for thorough exploration.

opposite

car park

Continued

Beinn a Mheadhoin 610 m

public road

Beinn a Mheadhoin

Glen Affric 6

350 m
300 m
250 m

N

1 km

Loch Beinn

250 m

Loch a Chlaidheimh

300 m
350 m

Loch an Eang

Cont'd

Cont'd Plodda Falls 3

40

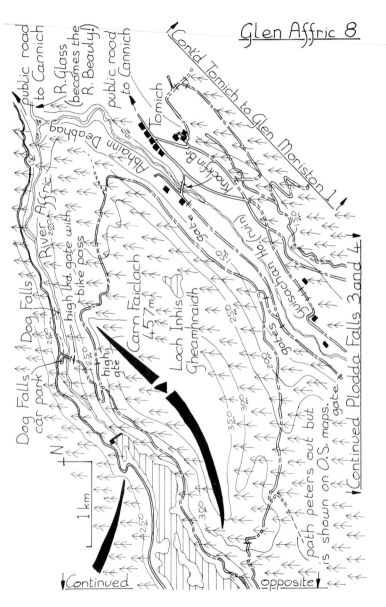

public road to Cannich

R. Glass (becomes the R. Beauly!)

public road to Cannich

Cont'd Tomich to Glen Moriston 1

Tomich

Knockfin Br.

Abhainn Deabhag

Dog Falls

River Affric

high lnd. gate with bike pass

high gate

Dog Falls car park

Carn Faiclach 457m

Loch Inihis Gheamhraidh

Guisachan Ho. (ruin)

Continued Plodda Falls 3 and 4

gate

path peters out but is shown on O.S. maps.

N

1 km

Continued

opposite

41

Easter Ross

Easter Ross

Access:- This area lies west and north of the towns and villages around the Beauly and Cromarty Firths. Access from the south is via the A9 which now uses the Black Isle as a stepping stone north of the Kessock Bridge, all routes dividing at Tore. However stretches of the old A9 via Beauly, and north of Alness, provide a more interesting drive north.

Accommodation:- In plenty around the Firths; there is a new SYHA hostel in Inverness, another at Strathpeffer, and Carbisdale Castle south of Lairg. Several campsites exist to the east of the region. Further north and west accommodation is limited to B.B's and the occasional isolated hotel.

Geographical Features:- An area of forest, wild moors and long glens with low watersheds enabling many of the tracks to interconnect giving a unique network of off-road routes unequalled anywhere in Scotland.

Mountains:- Ben Wyvis, at 1046m is flanked by the off-road tracks of Torrachilty Forest and Glen Glass, the latter providing access for hillwalkers. Further north and west Gleann Beag penetrates the "Deargs", a range of hills centred around the 1084m Beinn Dearg. Again the tracks in these remote glens give hillwalkers access to the quieter approaches to these hills.

Rivers:- The region is drained by - south to north- the rivers Farrar, Orrin, Conon, Glass, Averon, Carron and Oykel. The crossing of the main tributaries of these rivers can pose problems in the wilder regions; careful study of the detailed maps and local prevailing river conditions is needed before contemplating long routes. The Abhainn Poiblidh between Glen Acholl and Duag Bridge is of particular note.

Forests:- The main forests are Torrachilty and Morangie; both provide excellent off-road cycling. Other, quite extensive areas of forest flank the eastern routes in the glens though only the above provide usable networks of tracks.

Lochs:- Lochs Fannich, Glascarnoch and Vaich have all been raised by hydro dams. Other significant lochs are Loch Glass, Loch Garve and Loch Moire.

Emergency:- The long through routes require a degree of fitness and experience, and either wild camping or the use of bothies for full exploration of the region. This is, of course, the attraction. Less experienced cyclists are advised to opt for out-and-back routes (distance to choice) or the easier, forested regions.

Glen Strathfarrar

- a special note

Possibly conspicuous by its absence from this guide Glen Strathfarrar is unique. This 27km or 17mile metalled road is controlled by a manned gate limiting the number of cars and times of access. A small gate is however always open for cyclists who may enjoy an almost traffic free ride to the head of the glen and back. As the road is metalled a detailed guide is hardly necessary; suffice to say that its omission is no excuse for the the intrepid cyclist to leave Strathfarrar out of his or her itinerary.

Glen Orrin

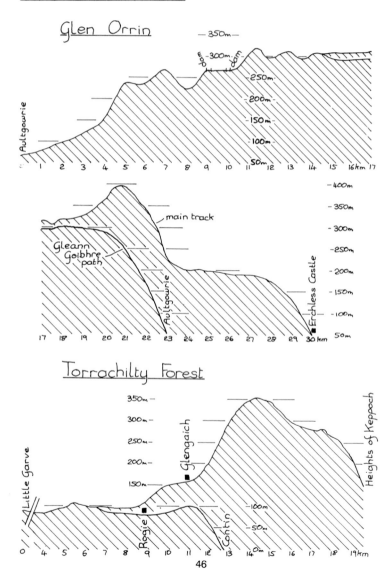

Torrachilty Forest

Strath Vaich/Strath Rannoch

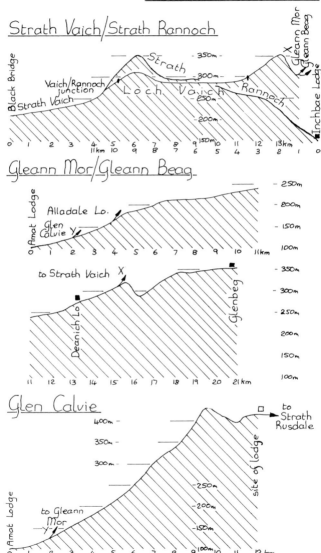

Gleann Mor/Gleann Beag

Glen Calvie

Easter Ross Routes 3

Strath Rusdale

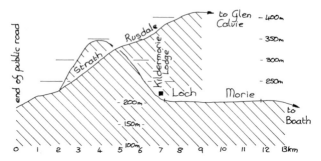

Glen Glass

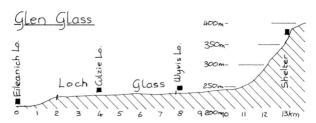

Strath Cuileannach

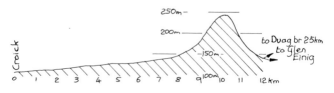

Glen Einig/Strath Mulzie

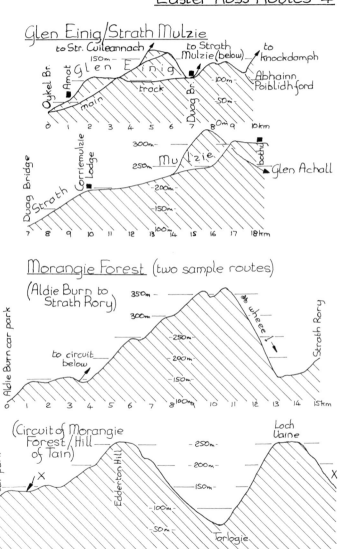

Morangie Forest (two sample routes)

(Aldie Burn to Strath Rory)

(Circuit of Morangie Forest/Hill of Tain)

49

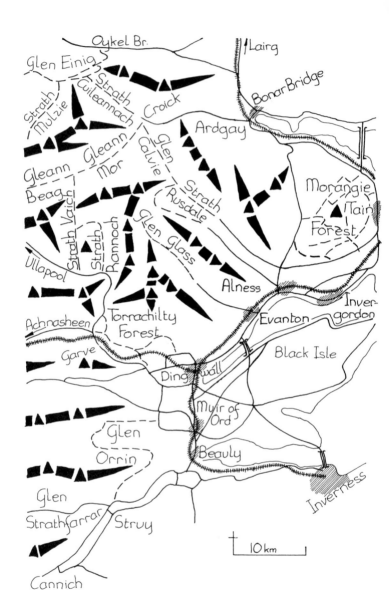

The Orrin circuit is best started from Aultgowrie, on the 'back road' between Muir of Ord and Marybank. The climb to the dam is metalled, giving a superb long off-road high level traverse and descent - to Erchless. A network of old paths around Gleann Goibhre links ruined farms. There is (rough) shelter as shown on the maps. One way Aultgowrie to Erchless is 29km (18m) and the complete circuit, via Beauly, is 54km (34m). A very satisfying route that "goes somewhere" rather than returning by the same glen. Great!!

Strath Conon

Moy Br.

beware! - high locked gate - kissing gate too small for bikes - and a cattle grid!!

Marybank

M. of O.

50 m

Fairburn House

River Orrin

150

100

N

1 km

Continued Glen Orrin 3

preferred approach (avoids the environs of Fairburn Ho)

Falls of Orrin

gate

Aultgowrie

150

200

start

Muir of Ord
5km / 3m

Gleann Goibhre (path)

Allt Goibhre

51

Glen Orrin 2

Since the building of the Orrin dams and the flooding of the lodge (near the head of the reservoir), the head of Glen Orrin has become a very remote place indeed. Access to these upper reaches is via Strath Conon; the reservoir shores are extremely rough going.

* I "speak" from bitter experience!

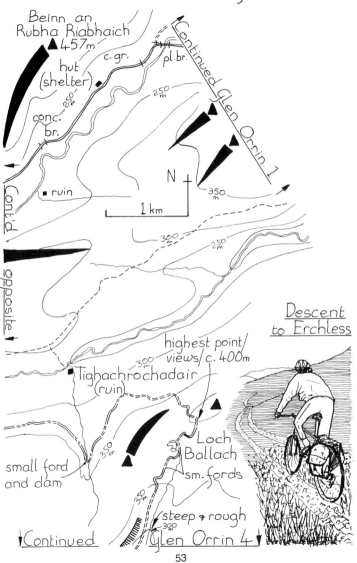

Beinn an
Rubha Riabhaich ▲457m

hut
(shelter) ◆   c. gr.   pl. br.

250m

Continued Glen Orrin 1

conc.
br.

250
m

■ ruin

350
m

N

1 km

300
m

250
m

300
m

highest point/
views/ c. 400m

Cont'd opposite ◀

Tighachrochadair
(ruin)

<u>Descent
to Erchless</u>

350
m

Loch
Ballach

small ford
and dam

sm. fords

300
m

steep & rough

↓ Continued   300
m   Glen Orrin 4 ↓

53

Glen Orrin 4

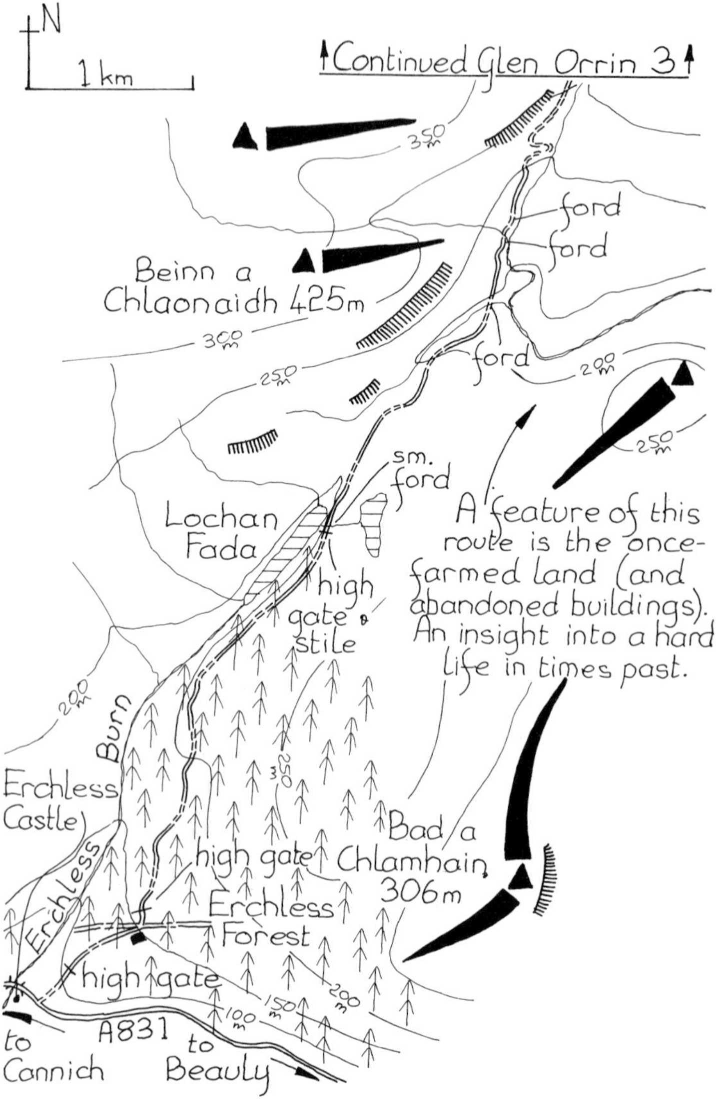

↑Continued Glen Orrin 3↑

N

1 km

350 m

Beinn a
Chlaonaidh 425m

300 m

250 m

ford
ford

ford

200 m

250 m

sm.
ford

Lochan
Fada

high
gate
stile

A feature of this
route is the once-
farmed land (and
abandoned buildings).
An insight into a hard
life in times past.

200 m

Erchless
Burn

Erchless
Castle)

350 m
250 m

Erchless

high gate

Bad a
Chlamhain
306m

Erchless
Forest

high gate

150 m
200 m

A831
100 m

to
Cannich

to
Beauly

Black Water
car/park
and loo.

picnic &
park

Little
Garve

Garve

conc. br.

gte

N

1 km

Heights of
Keppoch to
Contin on the
road is 10km or
6 miles. Take
account of the
climb up the main
road thro' Strathpeffer.
There is no shelter.

Loch
Garve

Black Water

iron gate

Centred around the forest
car park just north of Contin
the Torrachilty Forest tracks
extend from Little Garve to
the N.W. and to the Heights
of Keppoch, above the Dingwall
to Strathpeffer road. The Garve
to Contin section is designated
as a cycle route on O.S. maps
and serves as a (rather rough)
alternative to the busiest and
most tortuous stretch of the
A835 (using this road as a
return from/to Little Garve
is not advisable). The further
(Forest Enterprise) cycle
route to Heights of Keppoch
is best completed west to
east due to the amount
of climbing otherwise
involved. Return through
Strathpeffer on the
A834 is not usually
too busy. Little Garve
to Contin is 12km or
8m. Contin to H. of K.
is 15km or 10m.

Contd T. For. 2

55

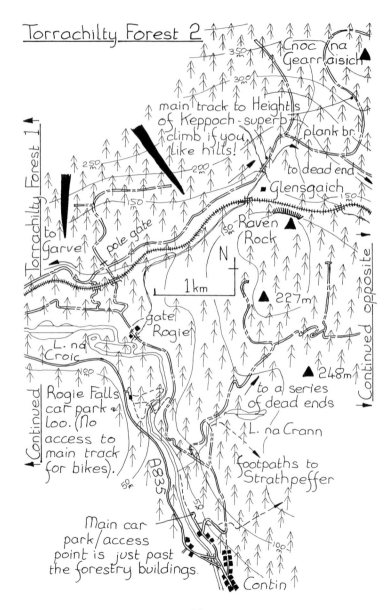

Torrachilty Forest 2

Cnoc na Gearr'aisich ▲

350m

300m

Torrachilty Forest 1 ◄

main track to Heights of Keppoch - superb climb if you like hills!

plank br.

to dead end

Glensgaich

250m

200m

150m

Raven Rock ▲

to Garve

pole gate

150m

N

1 km

227m ▲

Continued opposite ►

gate Rogie

L. na Croic

100m

248m ▲

to a series of dead ends

Rogie Falls car park & loo. (No access to main track for bikes).

L. na Crann

Footpaths to Strathpeffer

50m

A835

50m

100m

Main car park/access point is just past the forestry buildings.

Contin

◄ Continued

56

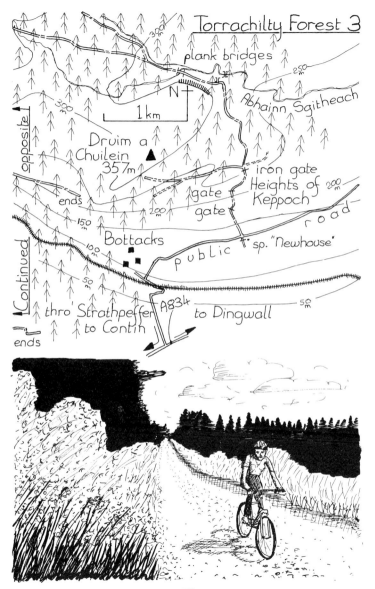

300

plank bridges

250

Abhainn Sgitheach

N

1 km

opposite

300

Druim a
Chuilein
357m ▲

iron gate
Heights of
Keppoch

200 m

ends

gate

200 m

gate

road

150 m

Bottacks

100 m

p u b l i c

sp. "Newhouse"

Continued

50 m

A834

50 m

thro' Strathpeffer
to Contin

to Dingwall

ends

The Strath Vaich and Strath Rannoch tracks provide access into the vast area of wild land north of the Ullapool road. Refer to Link Route 1 for details of exciting possibilities via Gleann Mor. That said, the trip to the Gleann Mor junction, just past the watershed, is worthwhile in its own right for a glimpse into this exciting region. There is shelter, 200 mts. from the track, at Lubachlaggan.

<u>Distances are as below:-</u>

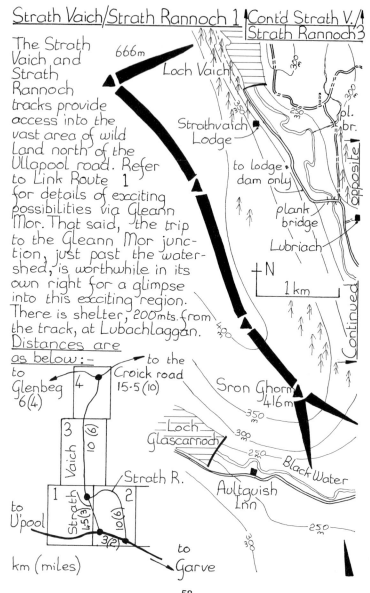

666m

Loch Vaich

Strathvaich Lodge

to lodge dam only

plank bridge

Lubriach

+N

1 km

Continued

opposite

pl. br.

300 m
300 m
350 m
250 m
400
300

to the Croick road 15·5 (10)

Sron Ghorm 416m

350 m

Loch Glascarnoch

300 m

250 m

Black Water

to Glenbeg 6 (4)

to U'pool

4

3

1

2

Vaich 10 (6)

Strath 4·5(3)

Strath R.

10 (6)

3 (2)

Aultguish Inn

to Garve

250 m

300

km (miles)

58

Strath Vaich/Strath Rannoch 2

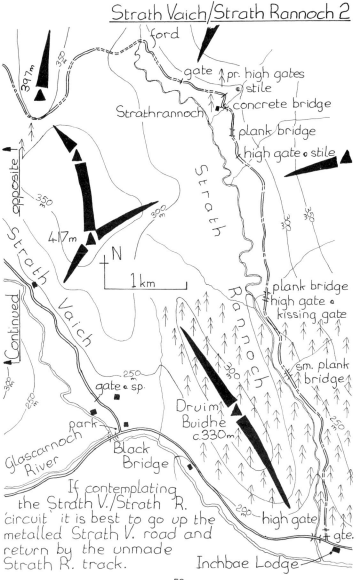

ford

gate ↑ pr. high gates
stile
concrete bridge

Strathrannoch

plank bridge
high gate • stile

397m

350

Strath

opposite ↑

350m

300m

417m

N

1 km

Continued

Strath Vaich

Strath Rannoch

350

350

350

350

plank bridge
high gate •
kissing gate

sm. plank
bridge

300m

250

250

250m

gate • sp.

Druim
Buidhe
c.330m

300m

250

park

Glascarnoch
River

Black
Bridge

200m

high gate

gte.

Inchbae Lodge

If contemplating the Strath V./Strath R. 'circuit' it is best to go up the metalled Strath V. road and return by the unmade Strath R. track.

Strath Vaich/Strath Rannoch 3

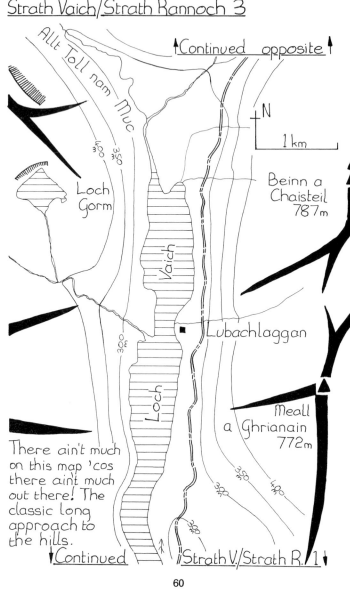

Allt Toll nam Muc

↑Continued opposite↑

N

1 km

400
350

Loch Gorm

Vaich

Beinn a Chaisteil 787m

Lubachlaggan

300

Loch

Meall a Ghrianain 772m

350
350
400

There ain't much on this map 'cos there ain't much out there! The classic long approach to the hills.

350

↓Continued

Strath V./Strath R. 1↓

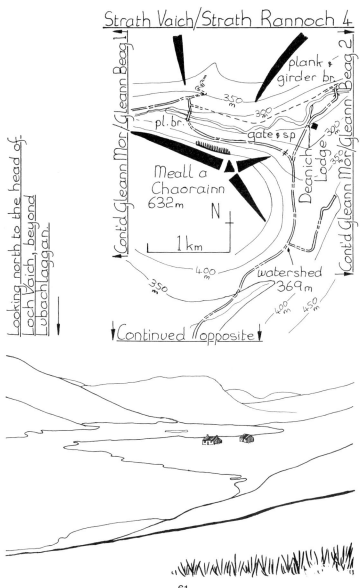

plank
girder br.

350 m

300

pl. br.

gate & s.p.

Deanich Lodge

350 m

300

Cont'd Gleann Mor/Gleann Beag 1

Cont'd Gleann Beag 2

Cont'd Gleann Mor/Gleann Beag 2

Meall a Chaorainn 632 m

N

1 km

400

350

watershed 369 m

400 m

450 m

Looking north to the head of Loch Vaich, beyond Lubachlaggan.

↓ Continued opposite ↓

Gleann Mor/Gleann Beag 1

Gleann Mor and Gleann Beag are accessible
from the minor road to Croick, up Strathcarron
from Ardgay. The start, from Amat Lodge, is
shared with Glen Calvie; thus Gleann Mor not
only links into Strath Vaich, but provides
continuous mountainbiking all the way from
Inchbae Lodge on the Ullapool road to Strath
Rusdale above Alness on the Cromarty Firth.
See Link Route 1 for all the many options.
Amat Lodge to the Strath Vaich junction
is 15·5km (10 miles) and Glenbeg bothy is a
further 6km (4 miles); the last 2km or so is
too rough with (not on!) a bike, believe me -
I've done it!! There is shelter at Glenbeg &
Alladale bothies, however Alladale is a hilly
and rough mile off the main route.
The start is on Gleann Mor/
Gleann Beag 4.

Loch Sruban Mora

735m

opposite

450 m

400 m vague but cairned X

350 m

vague

350 m

Glenbeg bothy (vague) vague

450 m shallow N vague furthest practical point for bikes

Continued

river crossing 1 km

X = green post

62

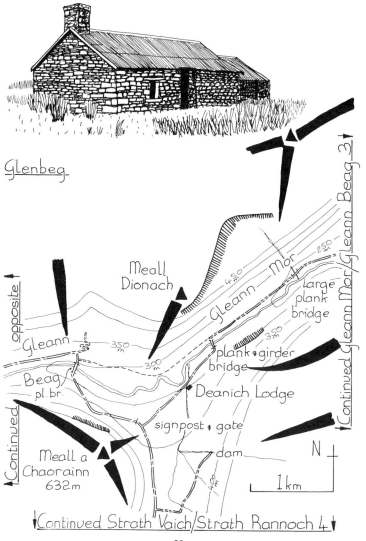

Glenbeg

Continued Gleann Mor/Gleann Beag 3

Meall
Dionach

Gleann Mor

large
plank
bridge

opposite

Gleann

350 m

300 m

250 m

plank & girder
bridge

350 m

Beag
pl. br.

Continued

Deanich Lodge

signpost & gate

dam

Meall a
Chaorainn
632m

400 m

N

1 km

Continued Strath Vaich/Strath Rannoch 4

63

Gleann Mor/Gleann Beag 3

The scene changes completely as the woods are left behind and the straight, narrow trench of Gleann Mor is entered. Deanich Lodge really is in an isolated location.

Stalkers' path into the wilds of Freevater Forest.

Alladale bothy

pl. br.

ford

636m

400

300

250

Glen Alladale

420

350

Sron Gun Aran 622m

lkd. shed

Mor

350 m

ruin

c660m

300

250 m

300 m

200

concreted ford

250

Gleann

400

shed

Abhainn a' Ghlinne Mhoir

concreted ford

400

Carn Feur-lochain 694m

Dunan Laith

691m

N

1km

opposite

Continued

Continued Gleann M./Gleann B. 2

Croick 2km

Amat Lodge

high locked gate ♦ high stile

+N

1 km

Alladale Lodge

259 m

Amat Forest

opposite

c.grid/bridge
planked bridges
gate

200

Gleann Mor

300

200

150

150

Alladale River

Glencalvie Lodge

Continued

▼Continued Glen Calvie 1▼

* Almost continued Strath Cuileannach 1

Alladale bothy.

Glen Calvie 1

Glen Calvie links the lower reaches of Gleann Mor with Strath Rusdale. The start, from Amat Lo. on the Croick road, is as for Gleann Mor and Gleann Beag. A left turn is then taken thro' the grounds of Glencalvie Lodge. This part of the route is intrusive, but *is* a right of way. Your author, being old-fashioned considers it a courtesy to dismount and wheel a bike in the close proximity of the lodge and surrounding cottages & outbuildings. This also makes it easier to speak to anyone you may meet..... Tearing along with an "I've a right to cycle anywhere" attitude doesn't help anyone!! - Certainly not the next cyclist! Amat Lodge to Loch a Choirn is 13km (8m), and 22km (14m) thro' to the public road in Strath Rusdale.

Continued opposite

Map labels:

Continued Gleann Mor/Gleann Beag 4

pole gte
pr. gts + c.gr.
pl. br
Glencalvie Lodge
to Gleann Mor/ Beag
iron gates
Cnoc na Ford Tuppat /438m
c.grid
gte . c.gr.
200 / 250 / 300 m
ft. br.
300 m
pl. brs. 350
350
Diebidale
pl. brs.
250 m
400 m
450 m
Glen Diebidale
300
N
1 km

66

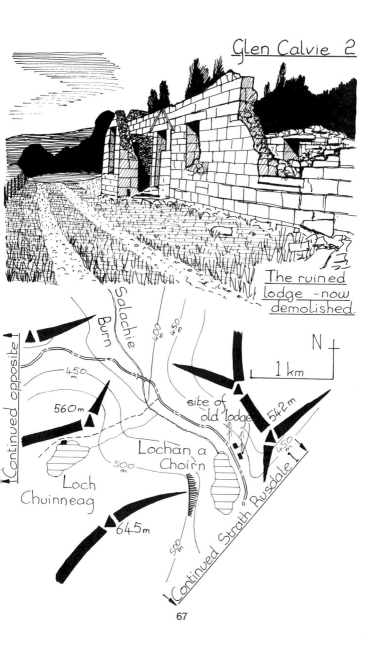

The ruined lodge - now demolished.

Salachie Burn

400m

450m

450m

Continued opposite

N

1 km

560m

site of old lodge

542m

450m

Lochan a Choirn

Continued Strath Rusdale 1

500m

Loch Chuinneag

645m

500m

Strath Rusdale 1

A minor road above the Cromarty Firth town of
Alness ends in Strath Rusdale at a car park.
From the road end a track continues some
19·5km (12m) to Glencalvie Lodge and a further
2·5km (nearly 2m) to the public road at Amat
Lodge, near Croick. An out-and-back ride
to Lochan a Choirn (9km/6m each way) or the
watershed before Glen Calvie (13km/8·5m
each way) is feasible. A further alternative
return (to Alness) involving some road cycling
is via Loch Moire, details of which are on
Strath Rusdale 3. Link Route
1 on page 138 illus-
trates how Strath
Rusdale fits into
this northern
network of
connecting
glens.

Lochan
a Choirn

Glen Calvie 2

Cont'd

522m

450 m

450 m

531 m

400 m

rocks forming road
block for vehicles
ruin

high gate • stile

opposite

Continued

N

1 km

68

Strath Rusdale 2

There is no shelter in Strath Rusdale or on the loop track around Kildermorie Lodge and Loch Morie.

Continued opposite

Abhainn Glac an t-Seilirh

350 m

plank bridges
high gate

Continued Strath Rusdale 3

516m

Bad a Bhathaich

350 m

N
1 km

concrete bridge

250

350 m

pole gate

300 m

Loch Bad a Bhathaich

Strath

Braeantra

gate
conc. bridge
park at end of public road

Black Water

Rusdale

200 m

to Alness
14km/9m

69

Strath Rusdale 3

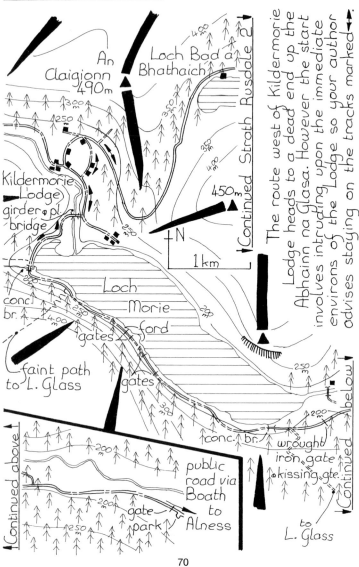

An Claigionn 490m

Loch Bad a Bhathaich

Continued Strath Rusdale 2

450m ▲

⊹N

1 km

Kildermorie Lodge
girder pl.
bridge

conc. br.

Loch
Morie
ford

faint path
to L. Glass

gates

gates

Continued above

public
road via
Boath
to
Alness

gate
park

conc. br.

wrought
iron gate

kissing gte.

Continued below

to
L. Glass

The route west of Kildermorie Lodge heads to a dead end up the Abhainn na Glasa. However the start involves intruding upon the immediate environs of the Lodge so your author advises staying on the tracks marked.

70

Glen Glass 1

The start of the Glen Glass track (on G.G.3) may seem a little intimidating; imposing lodge gates, barking dogs (big ones!), and the "estate office". However, this is a right of way and the trip up to the shelter - the limit for bikes and some 13km or 8 miles from the lodge - makes for a superb day out, almost in the shadow of the Ben Wyvis group of mountains. The shelter and the nearby waterfall is an ideal spot for lunch. Walkers' routes exist to Inchbae Lodge hotel on the Ullapool road, some 19km or 12 miles from the start; and also from Wyvis Lodge over to Loch Morie.

Beinn nan Eun 742 m

N

1 km

path peters out in the middle of nowhere!

ford

waterfall

the shelter

636 m

fords

ford

300

250

fords

shaky footbr. 20m up-stream

walkers' path peters out, but heads for a clearing thro' the forest above Inchbae Lodge Hotel.

Loch Bealach Culaidh

Queen's Cairn 645 m

Glen Glass 2

Continued

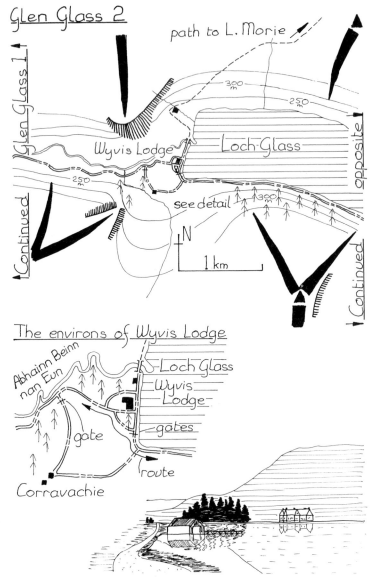

Glen Glass 2

path to L. Morie

Glen Glass 1

Continued

opposite

Continued

250 m

300 m

250 m

Wyvis Lodge

Loch Glass

see detail

300 m

N

1 km

The environs of Wyvis Lodge

Abhainn Beinn nan Eun

Loch Glass

Wyvis Lodge

gates

gate

route

Corravachie

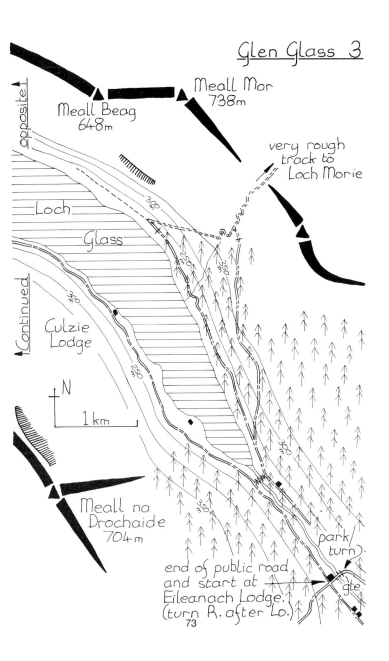

Glen Glass 3

Meall Mor
738m

Meall Beag
648m

↑ opposite ↑

very rough
track to
Loch Morie

Loch

Glass

Continued

350

350

350

Culzie
Lodge

350

350

N

1km

350

Meall na
Drochaide
704m

350

park/
turn

gte.

end of public road
and start at →
Eileanach Lodge.
(turn R. after Lo.)

73

Strath Cuileannach 1

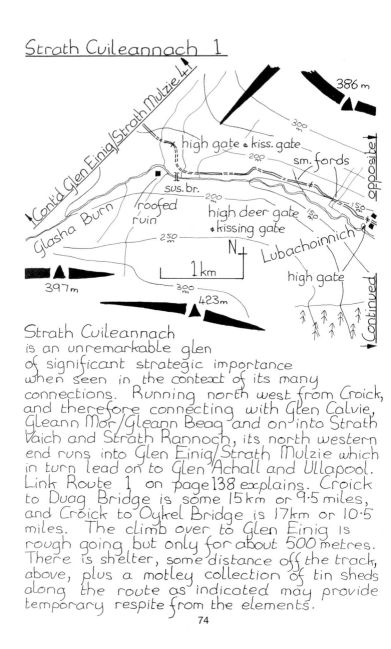

386 m

Cont'd Glen Einig/Strath Mulzie 41

high gate • kiss. gate

sm. fords

sus. br.

roofed ruin

high deer gate
• kissing gate

Glasha Burn

N

1 km

Lubachoinnich

high gate

opposite

Continued

397m

423m

Strath Cuileannach
is an unremarkable glen
of significant strategic importance
when seen in the context of its many
connections. Running north west from Croick,
and therefore connecting with Glen Calvie,
Gleann Mór/Gleann Beag and on into Strath
Vaich and Strath Rannoch, its north western
end runs into Glen Einig/Strath Mulzie which
in turn lead on to Glen Achall and Ullapool.
Link Route 1 on page 138 explains. Croick
to Duag Bridge is some 15km or 9.5 miles,
and Croick to Oykel Bridge is 17km or 10.5
miles. The climb over to Glen Einig is
rough going but only for about 500 metres.
There is shelter, some distance off the track,
above, plus a motley collection of tin sheds
along the route as indicated may provide
temporary respite from the elements.

Strath Cuileannach 2

Croick church

484 m

481 m

opposite ↑

Continued ↓

gate
concrete br.
tin shed
old fm. bldgs.
gate

gate
tin shed
concrete br.
gate
shed
gate
c. grid gate

Strath Cuileannach

250
200
150 m
150
200
250
300

↑N
1 km

Abhainn an t-Strath
Chuileannaich

557m

tin sheds

high gate
park

Croick

Croick Church

Glen Einig/Strath Mulzie 1

Glen Einig and Strath Mulzie combine to provide one of the most exciting routes in the area. Glen Einig ties together Oykel Bridge - at its start, on Glen E./ Strath M. 4 - Strath Cuileannach; and has important connections with Glen Achall - the thro' route to Ullapool on the

Continued Glen Achall 4.

Mullach a Bhrian Leitir

350 m

Glen Duchray

300 m

1 km

350 ft

Lochan Badan Glaslaith

N

400

450 m

Continued opposite

ends

Meall nam Bradham 677m

480

west coast. Link Route 1 refers. The afforestation at the start gives way to a wild glen under the northern crags of one of the remotest mountains in Scotland - Seana Bhraigh. Coiremor, a small bothy, nestles at its foot. Several small fords, one large ford (avoidable by a bridge), and one seriously large ford have to be negotiated in order to reach the bothy. A suspension bridge (if you call two strands of wire a bridge!) avoids the largest fords. Your author prefers to paddle. Oykel Bridge to Duag Bridge is 7km or 4.5 miles. Duag Bridge to the bothy is a further 11km or 7 miles. There is shelter at Duag Br. and the bothy, Coiremor. Take care at those fords. This route is one of the best!!

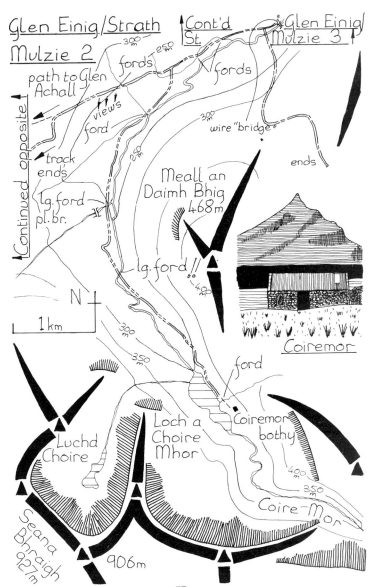

300 m

250

fords

fords

path to Glen Achall

views

ford

300 m

wire "bridge"

ends

260

track ends

Meall an Daimh Bhig 468m

lg. ford pl. br.

lg. ford !!

400

Continued opposite

N

1 km

300 m

350 m

ford

Coiremor

Coiremor bothy

Luchd Choire

Loch a Choire Mhor

400

350 m

Coire-Mor

Seana Bhraigh 927m

906m

Glen Einig/Strath Mulzie 3

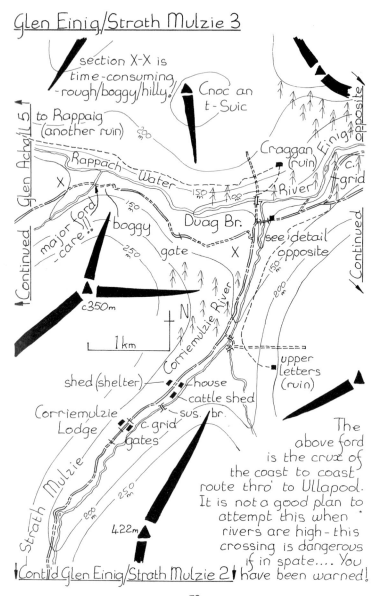

section X-X is time-consuming - rough/boggy/hilly.

Cnoc an t-Suic

to Rappaig (another ruin)

Glen Achaill 5

Craggan (ruin)

c. grid

Rappach Water

200

150

River Einig

opposite

X

150

Duag Br.

Continued

major ford - care!!

boggy

150

gate

250

X

see detail opposite

150

200

Continued

c350m

N

Corriemulzie River

1 km

shed (shelter)

house

cattle shed

upper letters (ruin)

Corriemulzie Lodge

sus. br.

c. grid gates

Strath Mulzie

250

200

422m

The above ford is the crux of the coast to coast route thro' to Ullapool. It is not a good plan to attempt this when rivers are high - this crossing is dangerous if in spate.... You have been warned!

Cont'd Glen Einig/Strath Mulzie 2

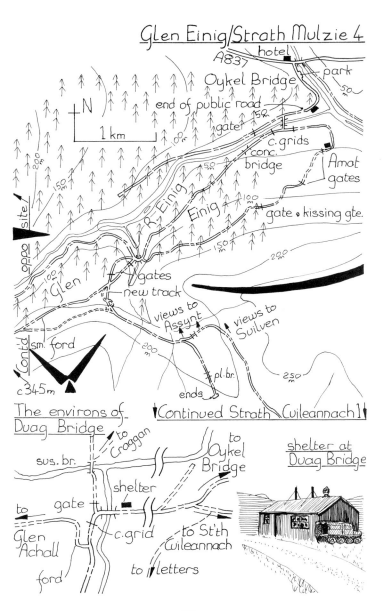

A837
hotel
park
50
Oykel Bridge
end of public road
gate
150m
100m
c.grids
conc. bridge
Amat gates
N
1 km
200m
150m
R. Einig
Einig
50
100m
gate • kissing gte.
150m
200
oppo site
Glen
100m
gates
new track
views to Assynt
views to Suilven
Cont'd
sm. ford
200m
250m
c 345m
pl. br.
ends

The environs of Duag Bridge

sus. br.
to Croggan
to Oykel Bridge
shelter
gate
c.grid
to Glen Achall
ford
to St'th Cuileannach
to letters

↓Continued Strath Cuileannach↓

shelter at Duag Bridge

Morangie Forest 1

Morangie Forest offers a huge variety, and several days out for the mountain biker. There are new forest tracks, older forest tracks, bits of old "roads" and several connecting stretches of minor road joining the various "entry points" to the forest. The tracks range in height from virtually sea level to over 1000'. Try to avoid cycling on the busy A9, though the A836 is not too unpleasant if used to connect the forest tracks. Distances are obviously to choice and a simplified(!) page plan/distance chart is set out below; distances are given in km only. The main car park is at Aldie Burn. The only shelter is at Coag.

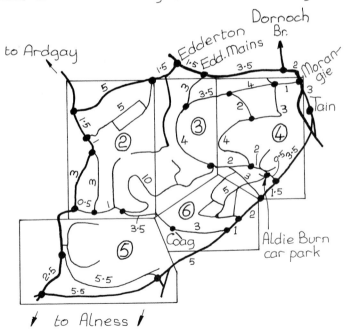

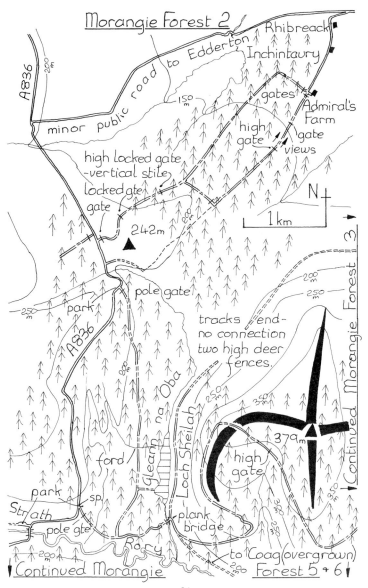

Morangie Forest 2

A836

200 m

to Edderton

minor public road

Rhibreack

Inchintaury

150 m

gates

Admiral's Farm

high gate

gate

views

high locked gate
-vertical stile

locked gate
gate

242m

N

1 km

park

A836

pole gate

tracks end-
no connection
two high deer
fences.

Gleann na Oba

Loch Sheilah

200 m

250 m

Continued Morangie Forest 3

250 m

379m

high gate

250 m

350

350

350

350

ford

park

sp.

Strath

pole gte

plank bridge

Rory

to Coag (overgrown)

200 m

Continued Morangie

Forest 5 + 6

280

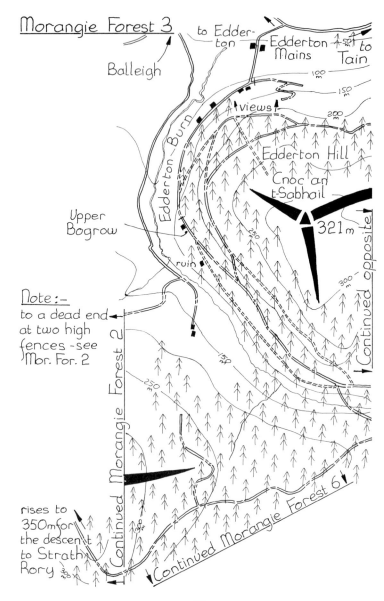

Morangie Forest 3

to Edder-ton

Edderton Mains

to Tain

Balleigh

Edderton Burn

100 m

150 m

200 m

views

Edderton Hill

Cnoc an t-Sabhail

Upper Bogrow

250

321 m

300 m

Continued opposite

ruin

Note :-
to a dead end
at two high
fences -see
Mor. For. 2

Continued Morangie Forest 2

150

250 m

Continued Morangie Forest 6

rises to
350m for
the descent
to Strath
Rory

300

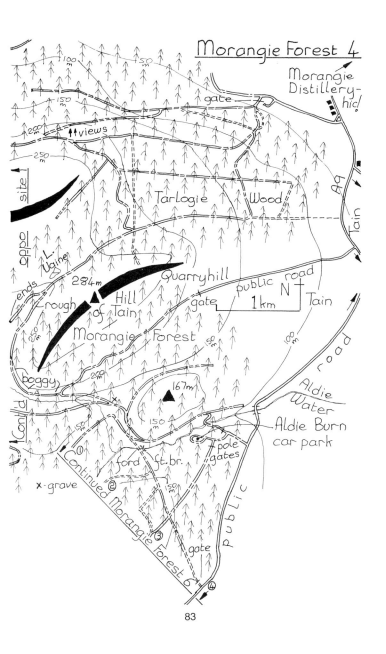

Morangie Distillery-hic!

Aq

Tain

gate

views

250m

200m

150m

100m

50m

site ↑

oppo

ends

rough

boggy

Cont'd

L. Uaine

284m

Hill of Tain

Quarryhill

Tarlogie Wood

Morangie Forest

public road

gate

N

1km

Tain

167m

Aldie Water

Aldie Burn car park

pole gates

ford   ft.br.

x-grave

Continued Morangie Forest 6

gate

public

①
②
③
④

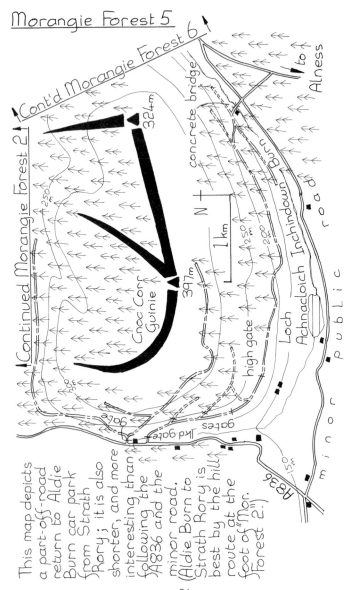

Continued Morangie Forest 2

Cont'd Morangie Forest 6

Morangie Forest 6

324m

concrete bridge

N

1 km

Cnoc Corr Guinie

397m

Inchindown Burn

to Alness

high gate

Loch Achnacloich

minor Public road

gate

3kd gate

gates

A836

A836

This map depicts a part-off-road return to Aldie Burn car park from Strath Rory; it is also shorter, and more interesting than following the A836 and the minor road. (Aldie Burn to Strath Rory is best by the hill route at the foot of "Mor. Forest 2".)

84

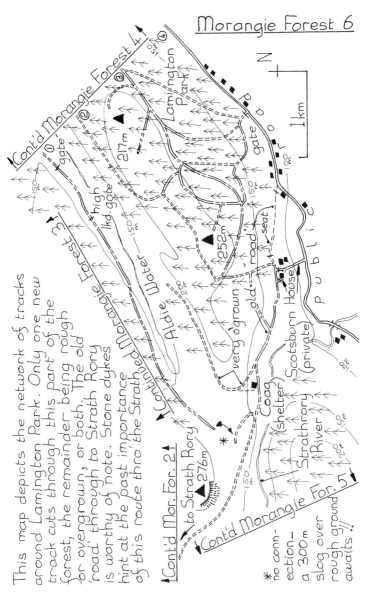

This map depicts the network of tracks around Lamington Park. Only one new track cuts through this part of the forest, the remainder being rough or overgrown, or both. The old 'road' through to Strath Rory is worthy of note. Stone dykes hint at the past importance of this route thro' the Strath.

Cont'd Morangie Forest 4 ↑

Cont'd Morangie Forest 4 →

① gate

②

③

④

217m ▲

Lamington Park

gate

Aldie Water

lkd. gate

6' high

Continued Morangie Forest 3 →

252m ▲

"old" "road"

very o'grown

seat

Scotsburn House (private)

Strathrory River

Coag (shelter)

* no connection— a 300 m slog over rough ground awaits !!

Cont'd Mor. For. 2 ↑

to Strath Rory 276m ▲

Cont'd Morangie For. 5 ↓

Public

N

1 km

Wester Ross

Wester Ross

Access:- This large and complex area lies north of Glen Shiel and south of Ledmore junction and Glen Oykel. It encompasses the western half of a huge tract of wild land crossed only by the Garve-Achnasheen and Garve to Braemore junction roads. Access is therefore a slow and tortuous affair; from Inverness via Garve and either the A832 or A835, or from the south via Shiel Bridge. The rewards are, however, proportional to the effort required to explore this exciting region.

Accommodation:- The most useful hostels are Ullapool, Torridon and Ratagan. A fairly even sprinkling of private hostels, bunkhouses, campsites, B & B's and hotels pepper the west coast, but inland even the main roads cross large remote areas with only the odd isolated B & B or hotel. There are many self-catering cottages on the coast.

Geographical Features:- A wild, indented, fjord-like coastline gives way to deep glens and high mountains. The watershed is well to the west so despite the location of the region much of the water drains to the east. There is little flat ground for cultivation.

Mountains:- Torridon, An Teallach, Slioch, Beinn Dearg, Sgurr Mor, The Five Sisters, Carn Eige.... far too many to single out the "best".... oh yes : The Fisherfield Forest..... I could go on (and on!), but (no doubt to your relief!) I won't. Suffice to say if you like mountains and wild country this region is a dream, if you don't you shouldn't be here... and why are you reading this ?

Rivers:- Almost a repeat of my notes on

Easter Ross as most are fed by or originate from burns in the west. Flowing west are the Rhidorroch River(in Glen Achall), Gruinard R., River Torridon, River Carron and River Shiel to mention a few of the main, albeit short, Atlantic-bound rivers.

Forests:- Apart from Gleann Udalain with its surprisingly good biking there is little forestry - hence generally fewer good mountain-biking routes given the huge extent of this region.

Lochs:- Here this area really scores! Sea lochs Loch Broom, Little Loch Broom, Loch Ewe, Loch Gairloch, Loch Torridon, Loch Carron, Loch Alsh and Loch Duich reach inland like fjords. Inland Loch Achall, Loch na Sealga and Loch Damh are all pleasant stretches of water whilst Loch Maree(formerly another Loch Ewe) is the finest, with its classic view of Slioch. A path alongside Mullardoch is included but Lochs Monar, Mullardoch and Affric belong with the eastbound rivers. Loch Fannich is a reservoir and forms a part of the Fannich/Glascarnoch/Vaich hydro scheme. Small "fishing" lochs abound - too numerous to mention. Fionn Loch is a wonderful sheet of water but the landowner has yet to be convinced that the word "access" also includes, by definition, cyclists.

Emergency:- Only three locations may give rise to problems for the unwary: The Glen Achall/Glen Einig connection which includes a major ford; the head of Loch Fannich which is very remote; and the Gleann Lichd/Affric connection which is both remote and hard going with a bike. Refer to Link Routes and study the page maps. Care is required!

Wester Ross Routes 1

Gleann Lichd

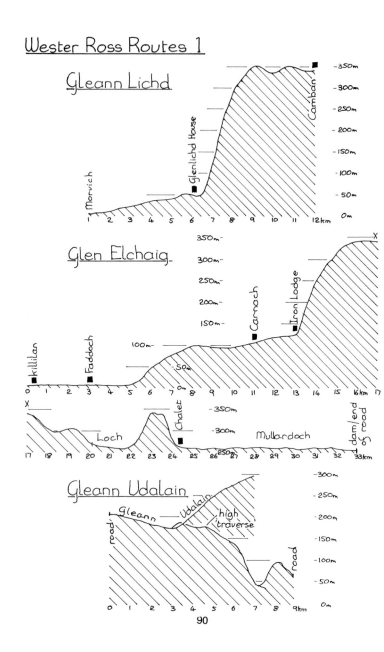

Glen Elchaig

Gleann Udalain

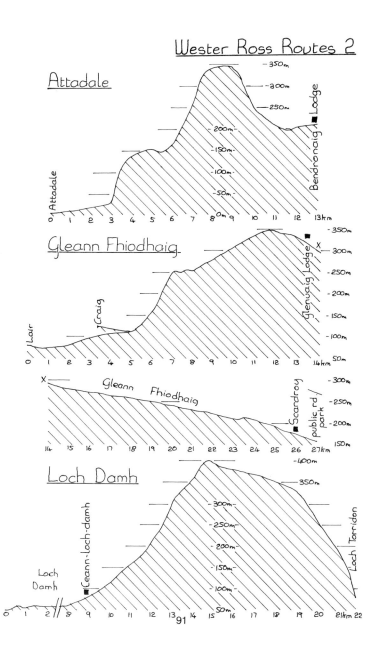

Wester Ross Routes 2

Attadale

350m
300m
250m
200m
150m
100m
50m

Attadale
Bendronaig Lodge

0 1 2 3 4 5 6 7 8 9 10 11 12 13km

0m

Gleann Fhiodhaig

350m
300m
250m
200m
150m
100m
50m

Lair
Craig
Glenuaig Lodge
X

0 1 2 3 4 5 6 7 8 9 10 11 12 13 14km

X
Gleann Fhiodhaig
Scardroy
public rd / park

300m
250m
200m
150m

14 15 16 17 18 19 20 21 22 23 24 25 26 27km

Loch Damh

400m
350m
300m
250m
200m
150m
100m
50m

Loch Damh
Ceann-loch-damh
Loch Torridon

0 1 2 3 4 5 6 7 8 9 10 11 12 13 14 15 16 17 18 19 20 21km 22

Wester Ross Routes 3

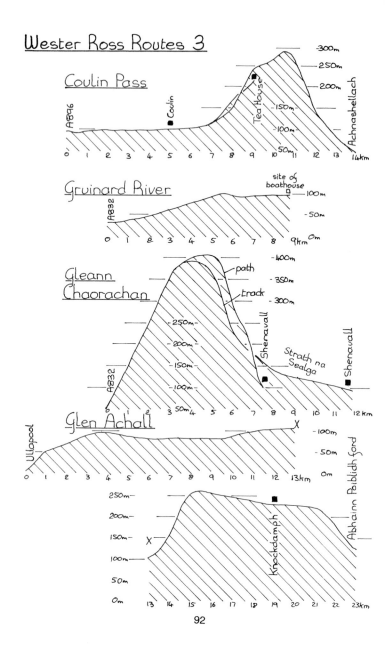

Coulin Pass

Gruinard River

Gleann Chaorachan

Glen Achall

Loch Fannich

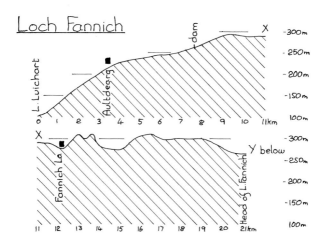

Lochrosque Forest

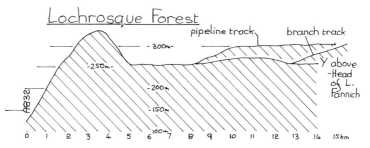

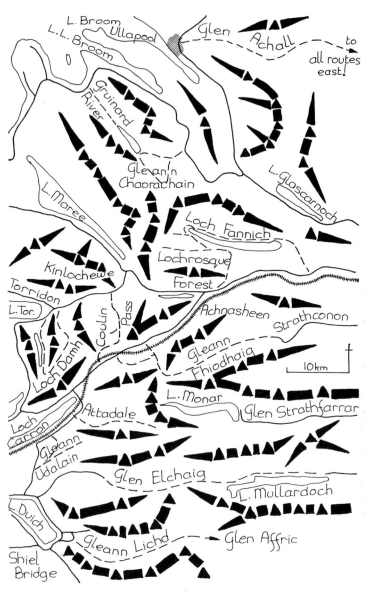

94

Gleann Lichd 1

Just north of Shiel Bridge Gleann Lichd cuts a deep trough heading in a south easterly direction behind the Five Sisters of Kintail to the bealach. Further north lie Sgurr a Choire Ghairbh, Meall an Fhuarain Mhoir and Ben Attow. Here it is possible to walk or cycle in the company of some imposing mountains. The glen provides a west coast connection into Glen Affric, the head of which is surrounded by even higher summits. The through route is, however, extremely rough to cycle - from Glenlicht House to about a mile west of Camban bothy - a distance of 4.5km or 3 miles -

best done east to west by bike. Glenlicht Ho. is a locked climbing hut with a tiny open bothy at one end. The next shelter is at Camban in Glen Affric. The start to Glenlicht Ho. is only about 6km or 4miles; half a day or an evening is ample time with a bike.

Glenlicht House

Gleann Lichd 2

The start is up a minor road just south of Croe Bridge sp:"to Glen Affric by Gleann Lichd or to Loch Cluanie by Gl. Lichd and An Caorann Mor".

Strath Croe

250m

100m

Croe

Croe Br.?

park gte

sp

sm. fords

River Croe

150

50

200m

Sgurr a Choire Gharbh
864m

891m

Meall an Fhuarain Mhoir
954m

sm. fords

50

Gleann

250m

Sgurr na 876m Moraich

N
1 km

concrete bridge

100

130

150

Lichd

280

sm. fords
gate

50

opposite

Beinn Bhuidhe
869m

Sgurr nan Saighead
929m

sm. fords

Continued

Sgurr Fhuaran
1067m

910m

Sgurr na Carnach 1002m

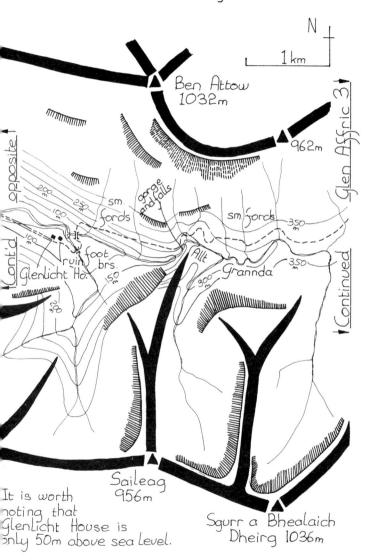

N

1 km

Ben Attow
1032m

962m

opposite ↑
Cont'd

Glen Affric 3

200
250 m
sm. fords
gorge and falls
sm. fords
350 m

100
100

Continued

ruin
Glenlicht Ho.
foot brs.
150

Allt Grannda
350

300 m

200
300

Saileag
956m

Sgurr a Bhealaich
Dheirg 1036m

It is worth
noting that
Glenlicht House is
only 50m above sea level.

97

Glen Elchaig 1

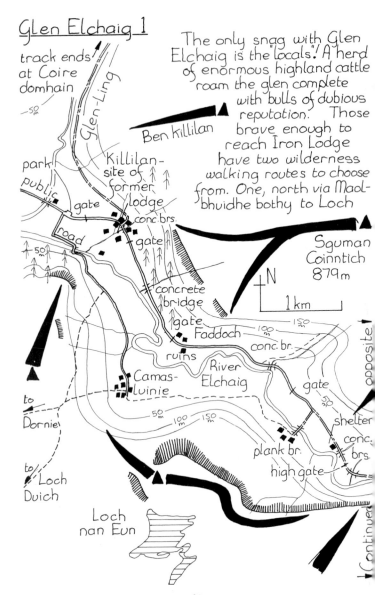

The only snag with Glen Elchaig is the "locals". A herd of enormous highland cattle roam the glen complete with bulls of dubious reputation. Those brave enough to reach Iron Lodge have two wilderness walking routes to choose from. One, north via Maol-bhuidhe bothy to Loch

track ends at Coire domhain

Glen-Ling

Ben killilan

park

public

road

gate

Killilan-site of former lodge

conc. brs.

gate

concrete bridge

gate

Faddoch

conc. br.

ruins

River Elchaig

Camas-luinie

gate

shelter

conc. brs.

plank br.

high gate

Sguman Coinntich 879m

N

1 km

to Dornie

to Loch Duich

Loch nan Eun

opposite

Continued

98

Monar, the second, due west tracing a vague stalkers' path north of the head of Loch Mullardoch, then by an even rougher path along the north shore to the dam. Iron Lodge is 13km (8m) from Killilan, Mullardoch dam is a further 21km or 13 miles.

Heavy-duty seat!

410m

N

1 km

Loch na

Leitreach

opposite

Continued

Continued Glen Elchaig

150 200

50m

150 100m

200m

730m

Falls of Glomach

Note:- The path to Strath Croe via the Falls of Glomach.

path to Strath Croe

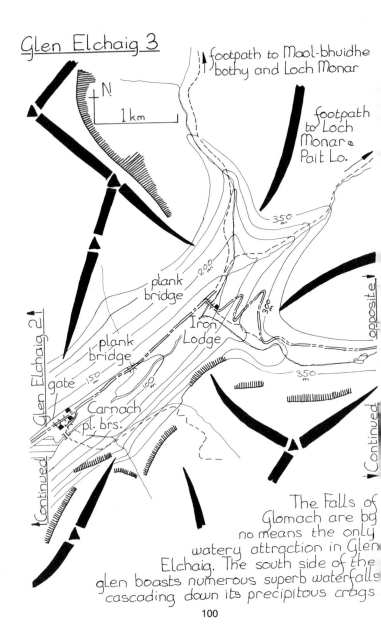

Glen Elchaig 3

footpath to Maol-bhuidhe bothy and Loch Monar

footpath to Loch Monar & Pait Lo.

N

1 km

350 m

200 m

plank bridge

Iron Lodge

30 m

Glen Elchaig 2 ↑

plank bridge

gate   150 m

100 m

Carnach   pl. brs.

350 m

opposite →

← Continued

Continued →

The Falls of Glomach are by no means the only watery attraction in Glen Elchaig. The south side of the glen boasts numerous superb waterfalls cascading down its precipitous crags

100

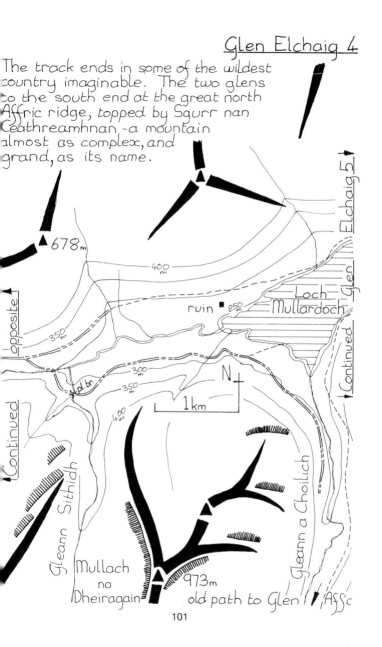

The track ends in some of the wildest
country imaginable. The two glens
to the south end at the great north
Affric ridge, topped by Sgurr nan
Ceathreamhnan - a mountain
almost as complex, and
grand, as its name.

Glen Elchaig 5

▲ 678m

400 m

opposite

Continued

Continued

350 m

ruin ■ 250m

Loch Mullardoch

pt.br.

300 m

350 m

400 m

N

1km

Gleann Sithidh

Gleann a Choilich

Mullach
na
Dheiragain

▲ 973m

old path to Glen Affic

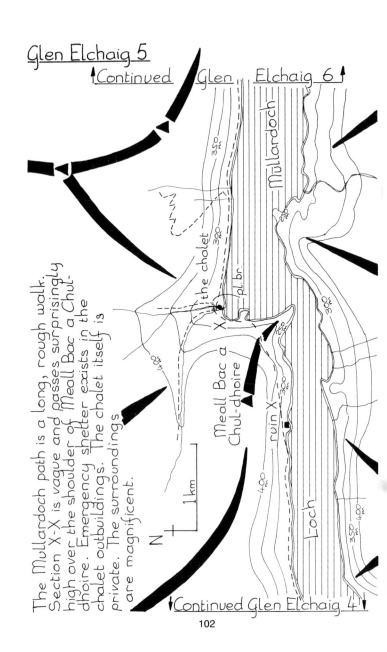

The Mullardoch path is a long, rough walk. Section X-X is vague and passes surprisingly high over the shoulder of Meall Bac a Chul-dhoire. Emergency shelter exists in the chalet outbuildings. The chalet itself is private. The surroundings are magnificent.

Mullardoch

the chalet

pt. br.

X

X

Meall Bac a Chul-dhoire

ruin X

Loch

N

1 km

350 m

300

400

350

300

250

300

400

400

350 400

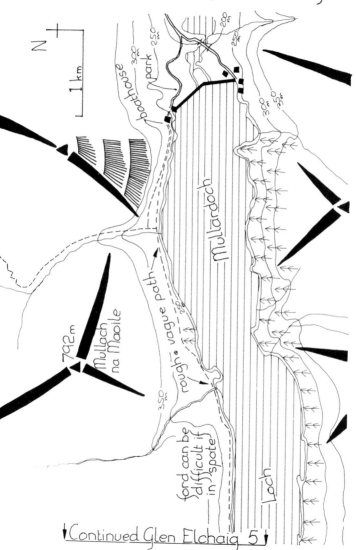

N

1 km

300 m
250 m
250 m
200 m
200 m

boathouse

park

Mullardoch

350 m
350 m

rough vague path

792 m

Mullach na Maoile

ford can be difficult if in spate

Loch

↓ Continued Glen Elchaig 5 ↓

103

Gleann Udalain 1

Ardnarff

Stromeferry

N

1 km

parking place
pole gate

park

pole gate

park

Brae
intra

c. grid

views

views

Meall
Ailean
322 m

park

high
gate

Gleann Udalain

park
pole gate
c. grid

This route has the rare
attribute of setting off down hill!

opposite

Continued

The Gleann Udalain tracks provide surprisingly good mountainbiking - much better than a casual glance at the O.S. map would suggest. The best starting point is probably point X on the map opposite. Gleann Udalain may then be explored to its limit, then a partial return brings you to the start of the high level traverse track -mostly downhill- so midge-beating speeds can be maintained throughout! The many dead-ends can be ignored and the track followed north to just above Stromeferry at point Z. The ride back up the road is a bit of a slog but this can be reduced by starting at the huge lay-by at point Y (thus spoiling that downhill start!) The round trip is 14km or 9 miles; the trip up to the head of Gleann Udalain adds 8km or 5 miles return. An ideal sortie for half a day or a summer evening. There is no shelter.

387m

c335m

opposite

ford

250 m

250 m

pathless right-of-way to Glen Ling

316m

N

1 km

Continued

Attadale 1

The track to Bendronaig Lodge initially follows the River Attadale (after passing the gardens) and strikes out over moors to descend to the Black Water which is a continuation of Glen Ling. However, the Glen Ling track is not continuous, ending at Coire-domhain. Bendronaig Lodge marks one of those wonderful wilderness "junctions". The pathless Glen Ling right-of-way meets the above track, and paths lead north to Bearneas (and eventually Gleann

Attadale House

cgrs

gate   cattle grid

Carn Ruairidh
378m

Strathan   locked gate   girder plank bridge

River Attadale

concrete bridge

363m

pl. br.

pl. brs.

opposite

Continued

335m   1km

N

Loch an Iasaich

better down than up!

106

Fhiodhaig via Bealach Bhearnais), and east
via Loch Calavie to Pait Lodge. Attadale to
Bendronaig Lodge is 13·5km or 8·5 miles.
There is shelter in the bothy at the lodge.

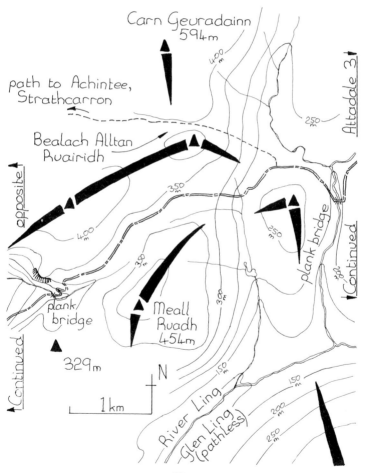

Carn Geuradainn
594m

path to Achintee,
Strathcarron

Bealach Alltan
Ruairidh

400

350

400

250

350

250

300

plank bridge

Meall
Ruadh
454m

300

329m

N

1km

150

150

River Ling

Glen Ling
(pathless)

200

250

opposite

Continued

Continued

Attadale 3

plank
bridge

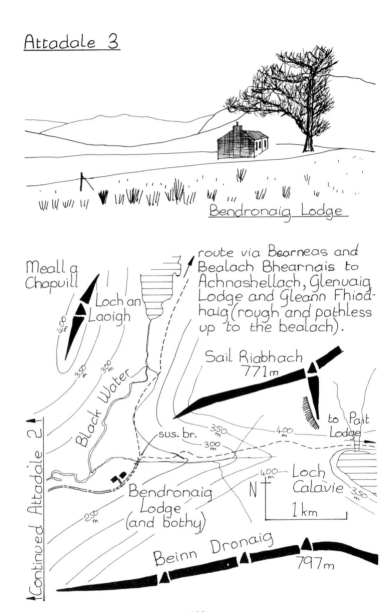

Bendronaig Lodge

Meall a Chapuill

Loch an Laoigh

400

350m 300m

Black Water

route via Bearneas and Bealach Bhearnais to Achnashellach, Glenuaig Lodge and Gleann Fhiodhaig (rough and pathless up to the bealach).

Sail Riabhach 771m

to Pait Lodge

350 400

sus. br.

300

350

N

400 Loch Calavie

350

1 km

Continued Attadale 2

Bendronaig Lodge (and bothy)

200

Beinn Dronaig 797m

Gleann Fhiodhaig 1

This route extends from Achnashellach in the west to the head of Strathconon. If cycling the best direction is from west to east as the climbing is done on good tracks, and the rough section (here a bike is more of a hindrance than an aid to progress) is covered with a slightly favourable gradient. Use of a bike east of Glenuaig Lodge cannot be encouraged in other than dry conditions due to erosion caused by cycle tyres; in the wet this section should be walked. The total distance from Achnashellach to Scardroy at the head of Strathconon is about 27km or 17miles. Starting at Craig saves some 5km or 3 miles. The 'short route' (one way) from Craig to Glenuaig Lodge is 10km or 6miles. Achnashellach has a railway station making a hard day out from here to Muir of Ord station a possibility - adding some 40km or 25

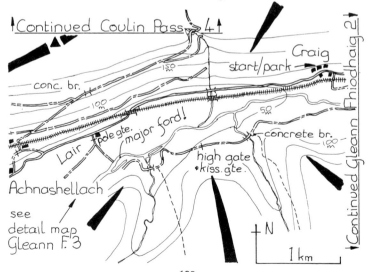

109

Gleann Fhiodhaig 2

Fhiodhaig 1 →

← Cont'd Gleann →

Meall an
Fhliuchaird
405m

300m

high gate
concrete brs.

conc. br

high gate, kissing
gate & s.p.

200m

250m
150m
100m
200m

miles of road
cycling to an
already arduous
day. The wide
but usually shallow
ford at Lair saves the
road walk/cycle to
Craig from Achna-
shellach station.
The only shelter
is an outbuilding
at Glenuaig Lo.
This route is
best kept for
a fine day!

sus. br.

450m
300m

450m
350m
350m

opposite →

← Continued →

single wire!

2-wire
bridge/
ford

350m

N

1 km

862m

Sgurr Choinnich
978m

Sgurr na Feartaig

Bealach
Bhearnais

path ends -
views to Skye!

pathless rough
route to Bearneas

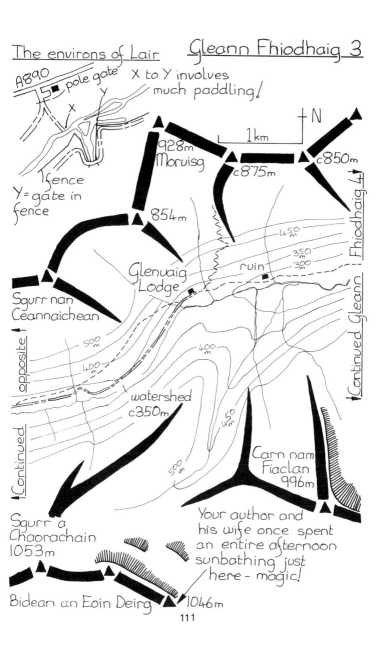

The environs of Lair

Gleann Fhiodhaig 3

A890   pole gate   X to Y involves much paddling!

fence

Y = gate in fence

X

Y

928m Moruisg

c875m

c850m

↑ N

1 km

854m

Glenuaig Lodge

ruin

450

350 m

300 m

Sgurr nan Ceannaichean

Continued Gleann Fhiodhaig 4

opposite ↑

500m

400m

400m

watershed c350m

450

500m

Continued ↓

Carn nam Fiaclan 996m

Your author and his wife once spent an entire afternoon sunbathing just here – magic!

Sgurr a Chaorachain 1053m

Bidean an Eoin Deirg

1046m

Gleann Fhiodhaig 4

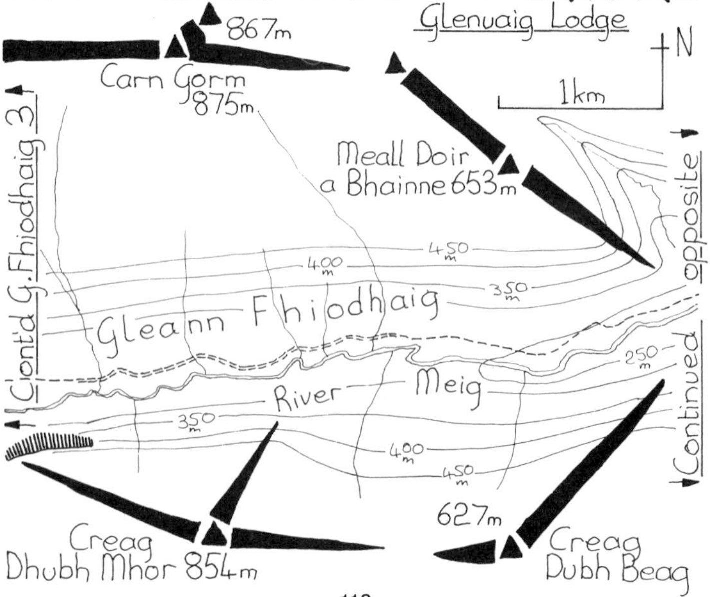

Glenuaig Lodge

N

1km

867m
Carn Gorm
875m

Meall Doir
a Bhainne 653m

Cont'd G.Fhiodhaig 3

Gleann Fhiodhaig

400 m   450 m   350 m

River   Meig

250 m

350   400 m   450

Creag
Dhubh Mhor 854m

627m   Creag
Dubh Beag

←Continued opposite→

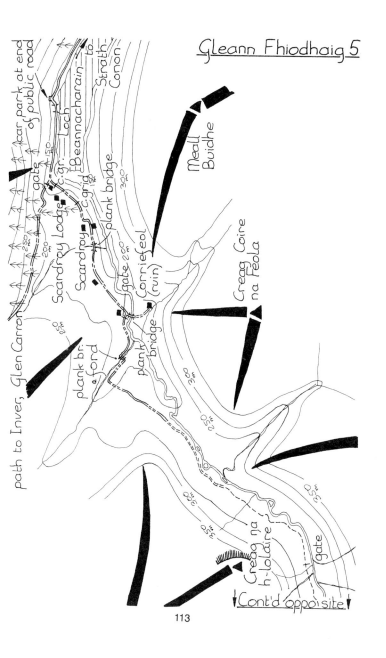

car park at end of public road

to Strath Conon

Loch Beannacharain

gate

150

S. grid

Scardroy Lodge

plank bridge

Scardroy

gate 200

150

Corriefeol (ruin)

Meall Buidhe

path to Inver, Glen Carron

250

200

250

plank br. @ ford

plank bridge

Creag Coire na Feola

300

250

300

350

250

Creag na h-Iolaire

gate

↓ Cont'd opposite ↓

113

Loch Damh 1

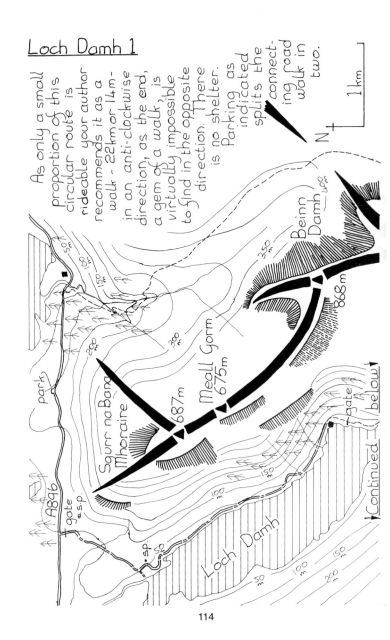

As only a small proportion of this circular route is rideable your author recommends it as a walk – 22km or 14km in an anti-clockwise direction, as the end, a gem of a walk, is virtually impossible to find in the opposite direction. There is no shelter. Parking as indicated splits the connecting road walk in two.

N

1 km

Beinn Damh 400

350

868m

Meall Gorm 675m

300

Sgurr na Bana Mhoraire

687m

200

park

A896

gate
s.p.

50

50

gate

s.p.

50

Loch Damh

50

100

150

200

100

150

150

100

50

◀ Continued below ▶

114

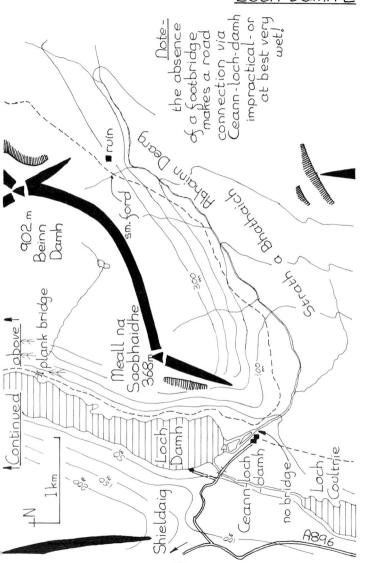

Note – the absence of a footbridge makes a road connection via Ceann-loch-damh impractical - or at best very wet!

Beinn Damh 902 m

ruin

sm. ford

Abhainn Dearg

Srath a Bhathaich

300 m

Meall na Saobhaidhe 368 m

100 m

plank bridge

↑ Continued above ↑

+N 1 km

Shieldaig

Loch Damh

Ceann-loch-damh

Loch Coultrie

no bridge

A896

Coulin Pass 1

The Coulin Pass links Glen Torridon with Glen Carron, running from Loch Clair (with its classic view of Liathach) in the north to Achnashellach Station in the south, a distance of some 14km or 9 miles. The track appears from the O.S. map to be continuous but the route is signposted around the path on the north east shore of Loch Coulin. This is an inconvenience for cyclists who have to wheel their bikes for about half of this mercifully short (about a mile) section. The track rises to its 286m summit just above Glen Carron, the northern half of the route being virtually level. A diversion to the tea-house and its neighbouring waterfall makes a superb lunch-stop. The best one-way direction to explore the Pass is from the south; out-and-back it is best from the north.

The tea-house

The environs of Achnashellach Station

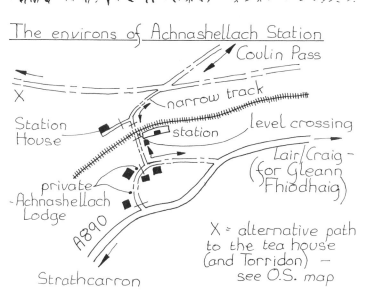

Coulin Pass

narrow track

X

Station House

level crossing

station

Lair/Craig – (for Gleann Fhiodhaig)

private – Achnashellach Lodge

A890

X = alternative path to the tea house (and Torridon) – see O.S. map

Strathcarron

Coulin Pass 3

to Torridon
A896

to Gairloch

Glen Torridon A896

park

A'ghairbhe

N

1 km

site of old bridge
pl. girder bridge

Carn Loisgte 446m

Loch Clair

100m

319m

views

planked br.
c.grid
Coulin Lodge

gate

route

150m

200m

gts ford
route ford

Loch Coulin

150m

Torran-cuilinn
lg. plank br.

gate

Meall an Leathaid Mhoir c515m

Coulin

River Coulin

200m

views to Beinn Eighe

Cnoc Daimh 344m

Continued opposite

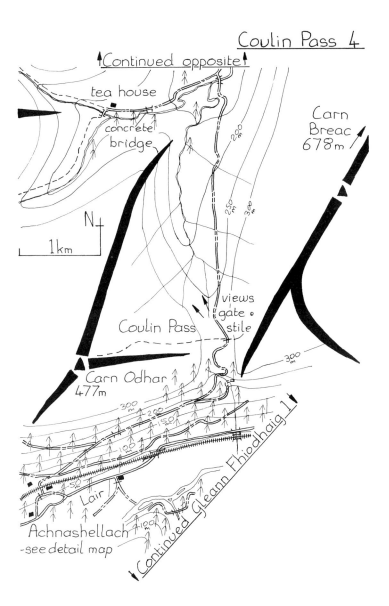

Continued opposite

tea house

concrete
bridge

Carn
Breac
678m

200

250 m

300 m

N
1km

views
gate
stile

Coulin Pass

Carn Odhar
477m

300 m
200
150

300 m

100

50

Lair

Achnashellach
-see detail map

100

Continued Gleann Fhiodhaig 1

Gruinard River 1

This track leads to the site of a boathouse at the outlet of Loch na Sealga, some 8·5 km or 5·5 miles from the road around Gruinard Bay. It provides a glimpse into the Fisherfield Forest - arguably our largest area of true wilderness. The track follows all but a few hundred metres of the Gruinard River. The fact that both the boathouse and the nearby suspension bridge no longer exist strengthens the feeling of complete desolation at the end of the track; a little used path continues along the south-west side of the loch to Shenavall via a huge river crossing!

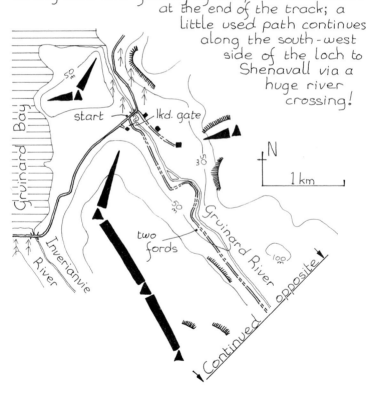

Continued opposite

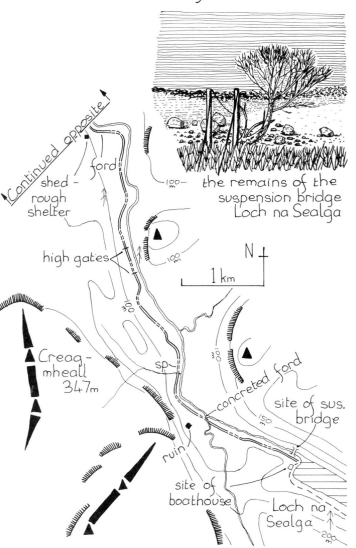

the remains of the
suspension bridge
Loch na Sealga

Continued opposite

ford

shed –
rough
shelter

high gates

100 m

100 m

N

1 km

100 30

Creag-
mheall
347m

sp

100 30

concreted ford

site of sus.
bridge

150 30

ruin

site of
boathouse

Loch na
Sealga

200 m

Gleann Chaorachain 1

The Gleann Chaorachain track provides another glimpse into the wilds of the Fisherfield Forest. Either as a return cycle ride to Achneigie, over a considerable climb, or as a walk visiting Achneigie and Shenavall returning over an often boggy path, the effort is well rewarded. The round trip via Achneigie and Shenavall is 19km or 12 miles. Achneigie is the halfway point. There is shelter only at Shenavall.

to Dundonnell

A832

locked gate

pk.

200 m

Glas Mheall Laith 960m

plank bridge

350 m

200 m

300 m

400 m

large ford

Continued

350 m

N

1 km

opposite

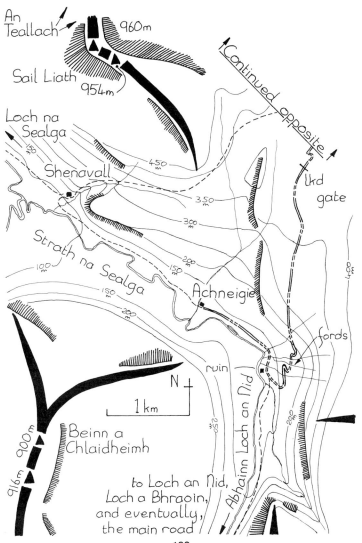

An Teallach

960m

Sail Liath
954m

Loch na Sealga

150

450m

Shenavall

350m

300

Strath na Sealga

200

100

150

Achneigie

150

200

Continued opposite

lkd gate

400

fords

ruin

N

1 km

Beinn a Chlaidheimh

900m

916m

250

200

Abhainn Loch an Nid

to Loch an Nid,
Loch a Bhraoin,
and eventually,
the main road

123

Glen Achall 1

The first mile or so of Glen Achall is spoilt by quarrying; indeed the track serves as the quarry road so beware of traffic. The start, thankfully, belies the remainder of the glen which is not only a gem, but as Link Route 1 describes, leads to a network of off-road glen tracks connecting west coast to east. The watershed is just above the south western end of Loch an Daimh but my "Glen Achall" describes the route through to Duag Bridge. Note the ford two km. west of Duag Br., and the underlined alternative walkers' path over to Strath Mulzie. There is shelter near East Rhidorroch Lodge, at Knockdamph bothy, and beyond the ford, at Duag Bridge. However in wet weather the ford may be impassable - walkers may then cut over to Strath Mulzie. Your author met several friendly horses and three very friendly pigs who tried to eat the bike tyres!

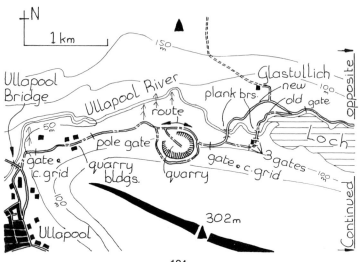

Glen Achall 2

Distances are given below from the centre of
Ullapool - the track starts 1km from "downtown"
Ullapool but there is nowhere to park here.

One way distance to:-

	km	miles
East Rhidorroch Lodge	13	8
Knockdamph bothy	19	12
Abhainn Poiblidh ford	23	14.5
Duag Bridge (via ford)	25.5	16
[Duag Br.(via Strath Mulzie)	27.5	17]
Oykel Bridge (main road)	32.5	20
Croick (via Strath Cuileannach)	40.5	25
Strath Rusdale (end of public road - via Croick & Glen Calvie	63.5	39.5
Alness (as above + public roads)	78	48
Black Bridge (via S. Cuileannach, Gleann Mor, Strath Vaich)	71.5	44 [1]
Inchbae Lodge (as above but via Strath Rannoch)	77.5	48 [2]

Return to Ullapool by main road, add: [1] 38.5 24
[2] 41.5 26

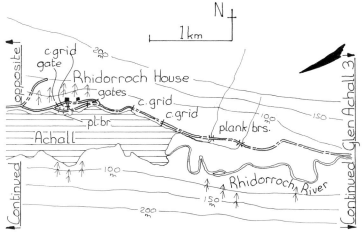

N

1 km

c.grid
gate
Rhidorroch House
gates
opposite
c. grid
c.grid
plank brs.
pl·br.
Achall
100
m
Rhidorroch River
100 m
150 m
200 m
Continued
Continued Glen Achall 3

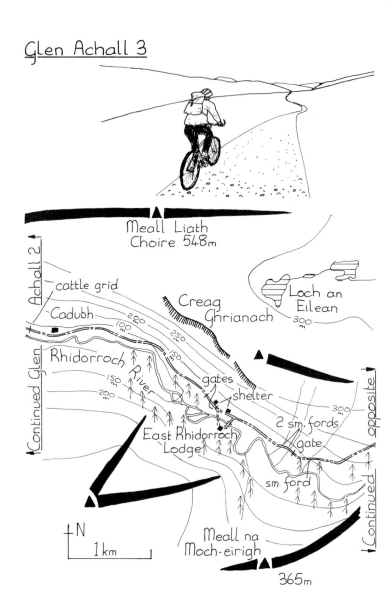

Glen Achall 3

Meall Liath Choire 548m

cattle grid

Cadubh

Creag Ghrianach

Loch an Eilean

Achall 2

Continued Glen

Rhidorroch River

gates

shelter

2 sm. fords

gate

East Rhidorroch Lodge

sm. ford

Continued opposite

N
1 km

Meall na Moch-eirigh

365m

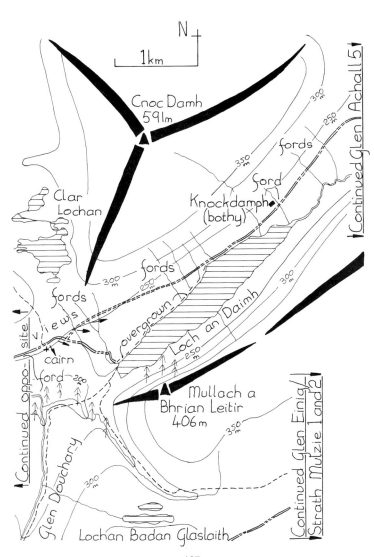

N

1km

Cnoc Damh
591m

Clar
Lochan

350m

300m

250m

fords

ford

Knockdamph
(bothy)

300m

fords

250m

fords

overgrown

Loch an Daimh

300m

250m

views

cairn

ford 200

Mullach a
Bhrian Leitir
406m

350m

300m

Glen Douchary

Lochan Badan Glaslaith

Continued Glen Achall 5

Continued Glen Einig/
Strath Mulzie 1 and 2

Continued oppo-site

Glen Achall 5

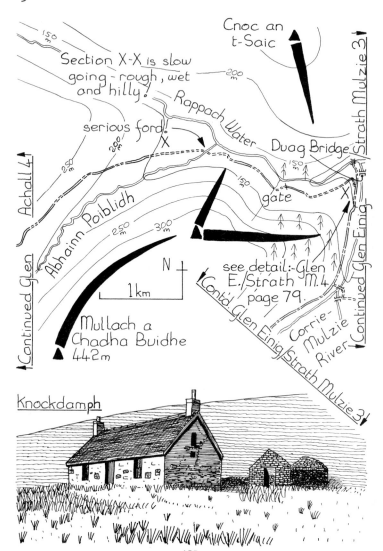

Cnoc an t-Saic

Section X-X is slow going - rough, wet and hilly!

Rappach Water

serious ford!

Duag Bridge

Abhainn Poiblidh

Achall 4

Strath Mulzie 3

gate

150 m

200 m

250 m

300 m

N

1 km

Continued Glen

Mullach a Chadha Buidhe 442 m

see detail:- Glen E./Strath M.4 page 79.

Contd. Glen Einig/Strath Mulzie 3

Continued Glen Einig

Corrie-Mulzie River

Knockdamph

The Loch Fannich 'track' is metalled for much of the way and as such makes for both tedious walking or a rapid approach to the hills by bike. The deteriorating track is **ride**able almost to the head of the loch. From this point a walkers' path climbs to a bealach at 560m and descends to Loch a Bhraoin and the main road 6km/4m south west of Braemore Junction. (*Note:-* if descending by this path be sure to cross the burn *before* it gets too big!). There is a tenuous connection to the Lochrosque Forest track, but see the note on page 137 regarding the gate on to the main road at the start, so a circuit of Loch Fannich is possible.

to Braemore

Nest of Fannich

400 m

An Sguman 739m

Cabuie La (demolished)

fords

pl. br.

350

300 m

350 m

N

1km

300 m

Abhainn a Chladh Bhuidhe

350 m

plank bridge

300 m

ruin

Loch Fannich

Beinn nan Ramh 711m

Cont'd Lochros- que Forest 3

Cont'd Loch Fannich 2

Loch Fannich 2

Fannich Lodge is some 12km or 8 miles from the start, and the ruin near the head of the Loch is a further 7km or 4.5 miles. The loop around the head of Loch Fannich and to the road/gate at the start of Lochrosque Forest track is 35km or 22miles. The distance back to the start of the Loch Fannich track (ie. road connection to road connection) is 12.5km or 8miles.

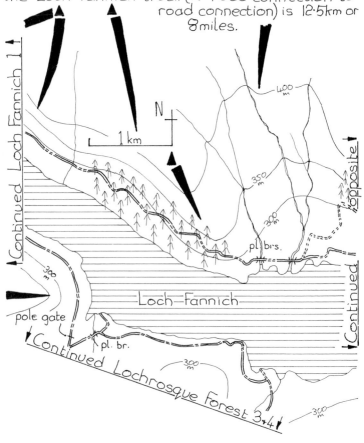

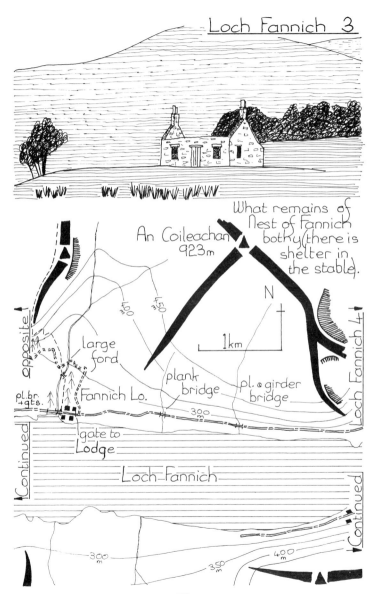

What remains of
Nest of Fannich
bothy (there is
shelter in
the stable).

An Coileachan
923m

N

1km

opposite

large
ford

plank
bridge

pl. & girder
bridge

pl.br.
+ gts.

Fannich Lo.

300 m

Continued

gate to
Lodge

Loch Fannich

300 m

350 m

400 m

Loch Fannich 4

Continued

131

Loch Fannich 4

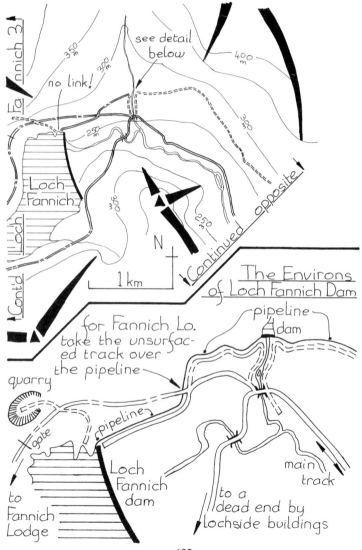

Fannich 3

350 m

300 m

see detail below

400 m

no link!

Fa

350

250 m

Loch Fannich

300

250 m

Continued opposite

N

Loch

Contd

1 km

The Environs of Loch Fannich Dam

pipeline

dam

for Fannich Lo. take the unsurfaced track over the pipeline

quarry

pipeline

gate

pipeline

Loch Fannich dam

main track

to Fannich Lodge

to a dead end by lochside buildings

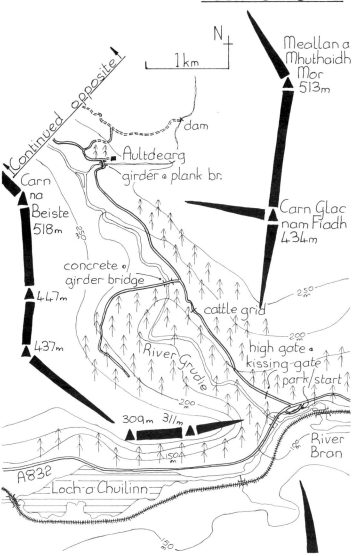

N

1 km

Meallan a
Mhuthaidh
Mor
513m

Continued opposite

dam

Aultdearg
girder & plank br.

Carn
na
Beiste
518m

Carn Glac
nam Fiadh
434m

350

concrete &
girder bridge

cattle grid

250
m

447m

200
m

River Grudie

high gate &
kissing gate
park/start

437m

200

309m 311m

150m

River
Bran

A832

150
m

Loch-a-Chuilinn

150
m

Lochrosque Forest 1

The Lochrosque Forest track used to lead to Cabuie Lodge, however the dam raised the loch, cutting off access to the lodge, but extending it to serve the pipeline. It ends in Strath Chrombuill - above the Heights of Kinlochewe. An even more recent track runs to the head of Loch Fannich and (just) beyond; see "Loch Fannich 1" for its continuation. Observant individuals will spot the old cast iron milepost, below, beside the track. The start is barred by a high locked gate, and fence, with unfortunately no stile - a rather unfair obstacle. The track quickly climbs to reveal Loch Fannich and explore some extremely wild country. The distance to the adit/dam above Strath Chrombuill is 15km or 9.5 miles; to the head of Loch Fannich is about the same, the junction being 9km or 5.5 miles from the start. There is no shelter other than a miserable concrete hut.

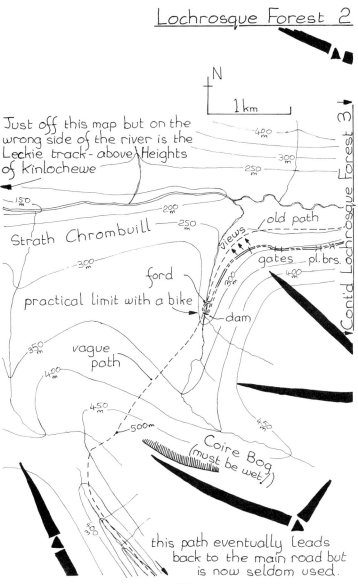

N

1km

Just off this map but on the wrong side of the river is the Leckie track - above Heights of Kinlochewe

400 m

300 m

250 m

Cont'd Lochrosque Forest 3

150 m

200 m

250 m

Strath Chrombuill

old path

views

gates   pl. brs.

300 m

400 m

ford

practical limit with a bike

dam

350 m

vague path

400 m

450 m

500m

450

400 m

Coire Bog (must be wet!)

this path eventually leads back to the main road but is now seldom used.

↑Cont'd Loch Fannich 1 & 2↑

Loch F.

Continued Lochrosque Forest 2 →

← Continued Lochrosque Forest 2

Continued opposite →

lkd. pole gate

400 m   450 m   300 m   350 m

pl. br.

pipeline

300 m

Strath

vague old path

Chrombuill

250 m

pl. br.

gate • dam   300 m   concrete hut (open shelter)

400 m

plank bridges • adits   350 m

Loch na Moine Mor

300 m

450 m

stalkers' path

N   1 km

933m
Fionn Bheinn

Note:-

The head of Loch Fannich is now devoid of
civilised shelter. Cabuie Lodge was demolished
before the dam was built, but the loch never
reached the site of the lodge as expected .....
(oops!!) . Nest of Fannich bothy, once a haven
in a wild and remote glen, was destroyed by
fire and is now ruinous, see sketch page 131.
All that now remains is the rubbish-strewn
stable next to the ruined bothy - but how
long will even this rough shelter remain intact?

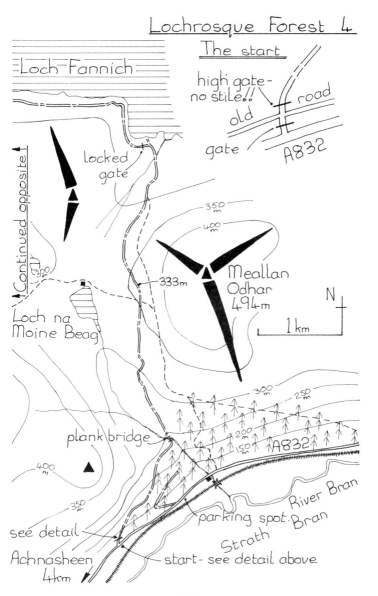

Lochrosque Forest 4

The start

Loch Fannich

high gate—
no stile!! road
old
gate A832

locked
gate

350 m

400 m

333m

Meallan
Odhar
494m

N

1 km

Loch na
Moine Beag

300

plank bridge

400 m

200 m
150 m A832

350 m

see detail

Achnasheen
4km

parking spot. Bran

River Bran

Strath

start— see detail above

Continued opposite

137

Link Routes

The link routes shown demonstrate how long through routes are made up from the various page maps. Variations can be planned using further adjacent routes but these should provide a basis for extended exploration.

The Northern Glens   Link Route 1

These northern glens form a unique network of linked tracks providing several options for off-road coast-to-coast cycling or long distance walking. The only snag is the return to the starting point, though Ullapool, Black Br./Inchbae Lodge all have bus services - as does Bonar Bridge - just down the glen from Croick.

Much care is required in planning long distance cycle rides or walks in this region. Accommodation is limited to bothies or preferably your tent. Use the route either as a loop between Alness and Black Bridge/ Inchbae Lodge or, via Croick, to Strath Oykel and on to Ullapool.

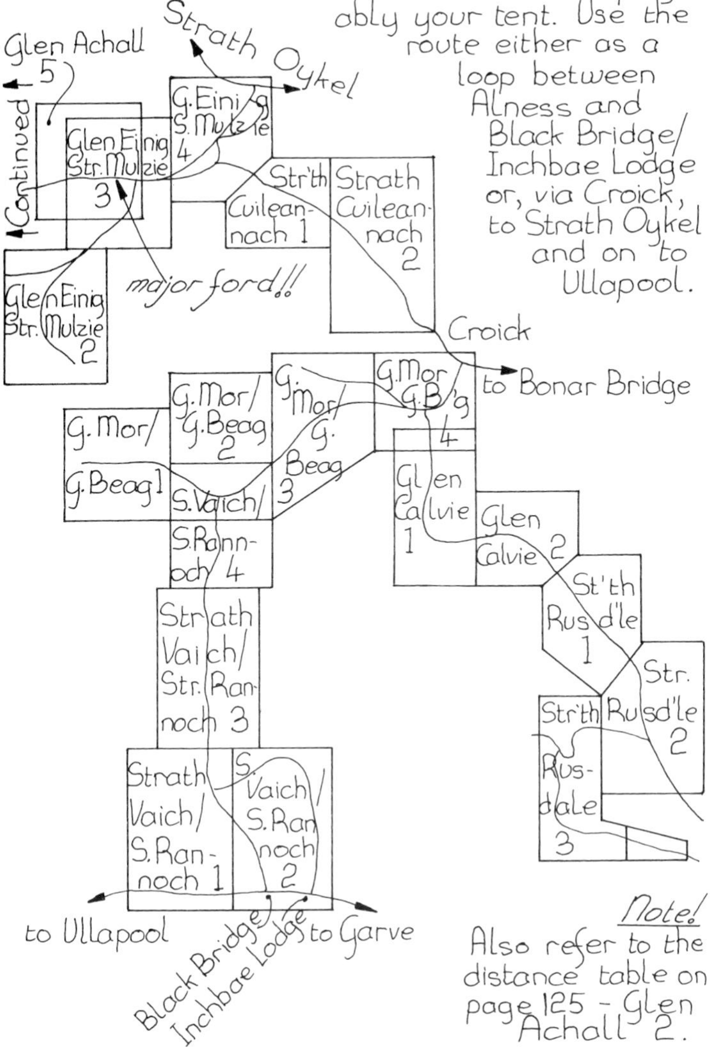
Strath Oykel
Glen Achall 5
Continued
G. Einig S. Mulzie 4
Glen Einig Str. Mulzie 3
Str'th Cuilean-nach 1
Strath Cuilean-nach 2
Glen Einig Str. Mulzie 2
major ford!!
Croick
to Bonar Bridge
G. Mor/ G. Beag 1
G. Mor/ G. Beag 2
G. Mor/ G. Beag 3
G. Mor G. B'g 4
S. Vaich/ S. Rann-och 4
Glen Calvie 1
Glen Calvie 2
St'th Rus d'le 1
Str. Rusd'le 2
Str'th Rus-dale 3
Strath Vaich/ Str. Ran-noch 3
Strath Vaich/ S. Ran-noch 1
S. Vaich/ S. Ran noch 2
to Ullapool
Black Bridge/ Inchbae Lodge
to Garve

Note! Also refer to the distance table on page 125 - Glen Achall 2.

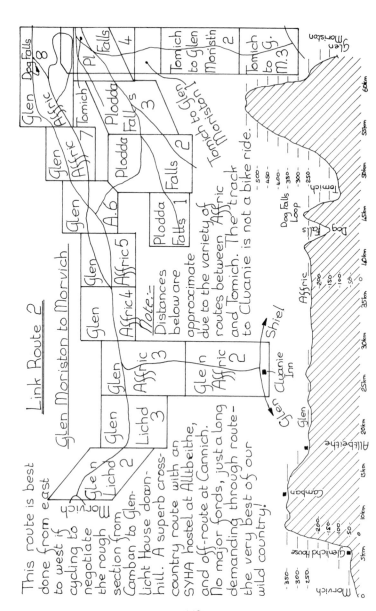

Link Route 2

Glen Moriston to Morvich

This route is best done from east to west if cycling to negotiate the rough section from Camban to Glen-Licht House downhill. A superb cross-country route with an SYHA hostel at Alltbeithe, and off-route at Cannich. No major fords, just a long demanding through route— the very best of our wild country!

Note:- Distances below are approximate due to the variety of routes between Affric and Tomich. The track to Cluanie is not a bike ride.

Glen Licht 2 · Glen Licht 3 · Glen Affric 2 · Glen Affric 3 · Glen Affric 4 · Affric 5 · Glen A.6 · Glen Affric 7 · Glen Affric 8 · Glen Dog Falls 8 · Plodda Falls 1 · Plodda Falls 2 · Plodda Falls 3 · Tomich · Pl. Falls 4 · Tomich to Glen Moriston 1 · Tomich to Glen Moriston 2 · Tomich to G. m. 3

Glen Cluanie Inn · Shiel

Morvich · Glenlicht House · Camban · Alltbeithe · Glen Affric · Dog Falls · Dog Falls Loop · Tomich · Glen Moriston

140

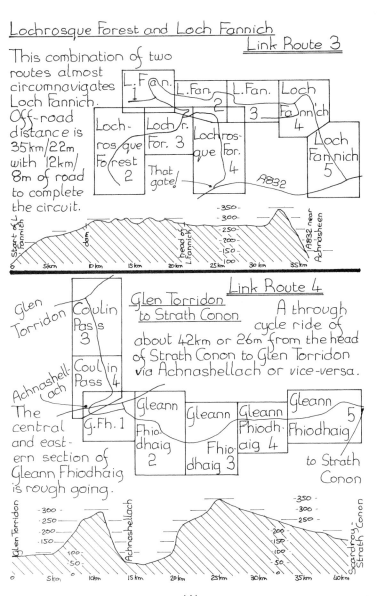

Lochrosque Forest and Loch Fannich
Link Route 3

This combination of two routes almost circumnavigates Loch Fannich. Off-road distance is 35km/22m with 12km/8m of road to complete the circuit.

L. Fan. 1 — L. Fan. 2 — L. Fan. 3 — Loch Fannich 4

Lochrosque Forest 2 — Loch r. For. 3 — Lochrosque For. 4 — Loch Fannich 5

That gate!

A832

Elevation profile: Start of L. Fannich — 0 — 5km — 10km — 15km — 20km — head of L.Fannich — 25km — 30km — 35km — A832 near Achnasheen. Contours: 100, 150, 200, 250, 300, 350.

Link Route 4
Glen Torridon to Strath Conon

A through cycle ride of about 42km or 26m from the head of Strath Conon to Glen Torridon via Achnashellach or vice-versa.

The central and eastern section of Gleann Fhiodhaig is rough going.

Glen Torridon — Coulin Pass 3 — Coulin Pass 4 — Achnashellach — G.Fh. 1 — Gleann Fhiodhaig 2 — Gleann Fhiodhaig 3 — Gleann Phiodhaig 4 — Gleann Fhiodhaig 5 — to Strath Conon

Elevation profile: Glen Torridon — 0 — 5km — Achnashellach — 10km — 15km — 20km — 25km — 30km — 35km — 40km — Scardroy Strath Conon. Contours: 50, 100, 150, 200, 250, 300, 350.

Well, that's it folks! Nine books and the series is complete. Anti-climax? Yes. Relief? Yes, at having stayed the course and not given up on what grew into an enormous task - a labour of love - but nevertheless my wife and I had to stick to the job in hand. Over the ten years or so we have enjoyed some 350 days in our wild places, spent around 50 days getting to and fro, and yours truly has written, sketched and drawn 1200 pages over 400 days. We have worn out two complete bikes, four pairs of wheels, eight pairs of tyres, two bums, smashed a dictation machine, yet only had one puncture (and yes, it was raining at the time!). My wife and I have each ridden over 7500 miles off-road (12,000 km sounds more impressive!) and walked a few hundred miles.... and all that's research - we walk, mountainbike and cycle for fun as well!

So, where are the best places to go off-road in the Highlands? My own choice of best centre, best glen/route and best link route book by book is as follows:-

<u>Book 1 The Cairngorm Glens</u>:- best centre, Braemar; best glen, Glen Avon; best link route, The Cairngorm Circuit.

<u>Book 2 The Atholl Glens</u>:- best centre, Blair Atholl; best glen, Glen Tilt; best link route, Glen Tilt/Glen Fearnach (or Tilt/Feshie - Book 1)

<u>Book 3 The Glens of Rannoch</u>:- best centres, Fort William or Loch Rannoch (near-not in!); best glen, Strath Ossian; best link route, Dalwhinnie to Fort William.

<u>Book 4 The Trossach Glens</u>:- best centre, Callander; best glen, Glen Almond; best link route, Loch Ard to Loch Tay.

<u>Book 5 The Glens of Argyll</u>:- best centre, Ardgartan; best glen, Glen Kinglass (Etive); best link route, Circuit of Ben Cruachan.

Book 6 The Great Glen:- best centre, Fort Augustus; best glen, River Dulnain; best link route, Dava to Rothes(or the Great Glen Cycle Route).

Book 7 The Angus Glens:- best centres, Ballater or Banchory; best glen, Glen Muick; best link route, the West Angus Glens(walking).

Book 8 Knoydart to Morvern:- best centres, Fort William or Ratagan(Shiel Bridge); best glen, Glen Kingie or Loch Garry; best link route, The South Glenshiel Circuit.

Book 9 The Glens of Ross-shire:- best centre, Cannich; best glen, Glen Affric; best link route, The Northern Glens - Alness to Ullapool.

The best places are, of course, those isolated glens, bathed in sunshine, with no pressure of time, reached through our own efforts no matter whether by bike or on foot, in the company of our choosing(or alone!)... Any of the suggested routes can provide, on the right day, all of this; it is there for the taking, free, wild and uncomplicated......

Incidentally, we have only once been ticked off by the-bloke-in-the-Land-Rover whose misguided interpretation of "access" differentiated between cyclists and pedestrians. "Bike or boots - what matter?" "They" will ban walking sticks next! Good manners always helps.

To sum up I must thank my publisher for his support in the task of producing and marketing these guides, and you, dear reader, for buying them! Thanks also to my wife for her untiring (except after a long day on the bike!) support, company and practical help(like feeding me). Hopefully, all this has resulted in many thousands of days out enjoying our wild places; if so, then your author is satisfied indeed with the completion of his self-imposed task.